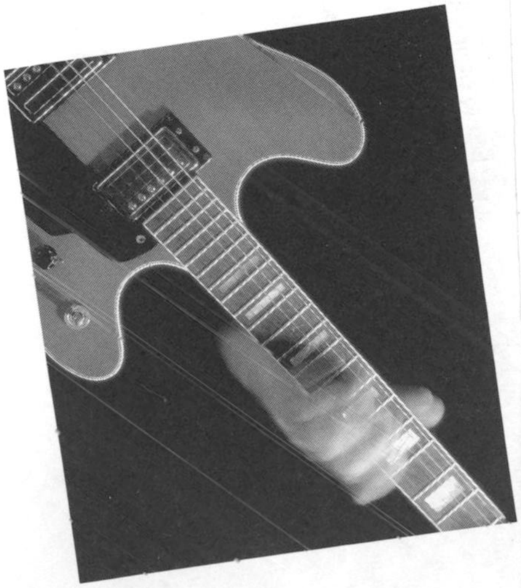

KT-152-219

THE ROUGH GUIDE TO

LEARNING
SUPPORT
SERVICES

Please return
on or before
the last date
stamped below

City College
NORWICH

Publishing Deta...

This first edition publi...
62–70 Shorts Gardens, Lo...

Distributed by the Penguin G...
Penguin Books Ltd, 27 Wrights La...
Penguin Putnam, Inc., 375 Hudson St...
257, Ringwood, Victoria 3134, Australia
Penguin Books Australia Ltd, 487 Maroo...
Penguin Books Canada Ltd, 10 Alcorn Avenue,
Canada M4V 1E4
Penguin Books (NZ) Ltd, 182–190 Wairau Road, Auck...
New Zealand

Typeset in Glasgow and Minion to an original design by
The Tipbook Company bv
Printed in The Netherlands by Hentenaar Boek bv, Nieuwegein

No part of this book may be reproduced in any form without
permission from the publisher except for the quotation of brief
passages in reviews.

The publishers and authors have done their best to ensure the
accuracy and currency of all the information in The Rough Guide,
however, they can accept no responsibility for any loss, injury or
inconvenience sustained as a result of information or advice
contained in the guide. Trademarks and/or usernames have been
used in this book solely to identify the products or instruments
discussed. Such use does not identificate endorsement by or
affiliation with the trademark owner(s).

© The Tipbook Company bv, 2000
128pp

A catalogue record for this book is available from the British
Library.
1-85828-650-6

THE ROUGH GUIDE TO
Electric Guitar
& Bass Guitar

Written by

Hugo Pinksterboer

ROUGH
GUIDES

THE ESSENTIAL TIPBOOK

Rough Guide Tipbook Credits

Journalist, writer and musician **Hugo Pinksterboer** has written hundreds of articles and reviews for international music magazines. He is the author of the reference work for cymbals (*The Cymbal Book*, Hal Leonard, US) and has written and developed a wide variety of musical manuals and courses.

Illustrator, designer and musician **Gijs Bierenbroodspot** has worked as an art director in magazines and advertising. While searching in vain for information about saxophone mouthpieces he came up with the idea for this series of books on music and musical instruments. Since then, he has created the layout and the illustrations for all of the books.

Acknowledgements

Concept, design and illustrations: Gijs Bierenbroodspot

Translation: MdJ Copy & Translation

Editor: Duncan Harris

IN BRIEF

Have you just started playing? Are you thinking about buying an electric guitar or bass? Do you want to know more about the instrument you already own? Then this book will tell you everything you need to know. You'll read about the names of all the parts and what they do, about lessons and practicing, strings and pickups, tuning and maintenance, and about the history and family of the guitar and bass. And much, much more.

Get the most from your instrument

Having read this Rough Guide, you'll be able to get the most out of your guitar or bass, to buy the best instrument possible, and to easily grasp any other literature on the subject.

Begin at the beginning

If you've just started playing, or haven't yet begun, pay particular attention to the first four chapters. If you've been playing longer, you might want to skip ahead to Chapter 5.

Glossary

Most of the terms you'll come across as a guitarist or bassist are explained in the glossary at the end of the book, which doubles as an index.

CONTENTS

1. ELECTRIC GUITAR AND BASS

Guitarists and bassists provide everything from flamboyant solos and power chords to gentle accompaniments and bass lines. There are endless types of guitars and basses, and just as many ways to play.

With an electric guitar or bass you can play lots of musical styles – from metal to jazz, from funk to folk. And with a guitar, like a piano or keyboard, you can play chords (more than one note at a time), making it ideal for playing alone as well as in a band.

Singer-guitarists
The guitar is one of the best instruments to play as a singer, as it can provide so many types of accompaniment, and many singer-guitarists perform whole concerts alone. There are lots of singer-bassists, too, such as Sting and Paul McCartney.

Bass playing
The bass, together with the drums, creates a band's foundation. But this doesn't mean just playing simple lines – modern bass technique includes everything from chords and slapping to slides and solos.

Popular instruments
Guitars and basses are very popular instruments – here are some of the reasons:
- You can pick up the basics pretty quickly. It can take just a few weeks to learn to play a number of songs.

- You don't need to learn how to read music if you don't want to – there are lots of famous players who can't read a note.
- It's not expensive to buy a reasonable guitar or bass. With a little patience, you can find a decent instrument and a small amp relatively cheaply.
- Guitars and basses are very portable, and you can even get amplifiers that fit in a rucksack.

Each instrument
There are millions of guitars and basses, and each has its own sound. However, that sound isn't fixed, as you can alter it by changing the strings or pickups, or by using different playing techniques.

Each player
You can strum or pluck the strings with your fingers or you can use a *pick*. You can also slap them or tap them, make them scream, or dampen them with the side of your hand. Each player uses their own mixture of techniques and creates their own sound.

Basses
Basses are more or less the same as guitars, only they sound lower and usually have fewer strings. Most have four, but basses with five, six or even more strings are increasingly common. These are great for playing solos and advanced techniques, but the more strings there are, the wider the neck has to be, and the harder some simple techniques become. For this reason, a four-string bass is the best type to start learning on.

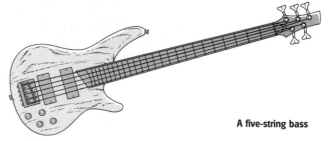

A five-string bass

2. A QUICK TOUR

A guitar or bass consists of many components. There's the body, neck and fretboard, usually all made of wood, but also loads of smaller metal and plastic parts. This chapter tells you what they're all called and what they do.

The sound of an acoustic guitar is amplified in its hollow body, which is also known as a *soundbox*. Electric guitars fall into two broad groups: those without a soundbox, *solid-bodies*, and those with a soundbox, *hollow-bodies*.

Pickups
The body houses the *pickups* and all the necessary wiring. As the name suggests, pickups literally 'pick up' the string's vibrations and convert them into electric signals, which are turned into sound by an amplifier.

Bass guitars
The electric bass is very similar to the electric guitar. The standard four strings of a bass are tuned to the same notes as the thickest four strings of a guitar – but one octave lower.

THE SOLID-BODY
Most guitars, and nearly all basses, are solid-bodies. These instruments come in endless different shapes and sizes, and many brands have very recognizable models – you can often tell from a distance what make of guitar or bass someone is playing.

3

SOLID-BODY GUITAR

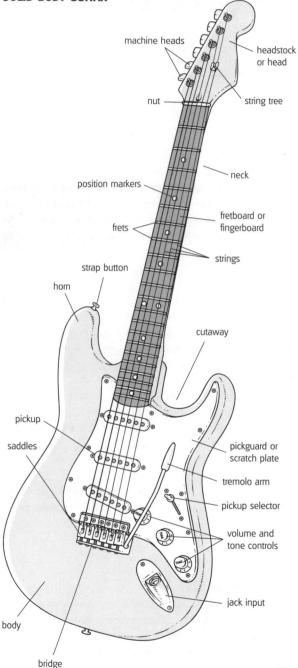

machine heads

headstock or head

nut

string tree

neck

position markers

fretboard or fingerboard

frets

strings

strap button

horn

cutaway

pickup

saddles

pickguard or scratch plate

tremolo arm

pickup selector

volume and tone controls

jack input

body

bridge

Cutaways

To allow easier access to the highest frets, most electric guitars and basses have a section of the body cut out – a *cutaway*. Many instruments have a cutaway on both sides of the neck.

Pickguards

A *pickguard* or *scratch plate* is a piece of plastic that prevents the body from being scratched by picks, and some manufacturers produce them in very distinctive colours and patterns. On many instruments, removing the pickguard allows access to the wiring inside the body.

The neck

The *neck* is the long wooden section of a guitar or bass that runs between the body and the headstock. To prevent the tension of the strings from warping the neck, it often has an adjustable metal rod built into it, called a *truss rod*.

Solid-body bass guitar

The fretboard

The part of the neck that runs underneath the strings is called the *fretboard*, or *fingerboard*. Usually it's a thin piece of wood glued to the neck, but on some instruments the fretboard and neck are one piece.

Frets

The *frets* are the thin metal strips that run across the fretboard. An instrument with frets is easier to play in tune than one without frets, such as a violin (and some basses). 'Playing the fourth fret' means pressing the string down between the third and the fourth fret, as close to the fourth as possible. Pressing a string to a fret is known as *fretting* or *stopping* the string.

Position markers

The space between two frets is sometimes referred to as a *position*, and most guitars and basses have dots or inlays on the front and side of the fretboard to make it easier to find the right position quickly. These are called *position markers*.

The headstock

The *headstock*, or *head*, lies at the end of the neck. There are many different types of head design, some unique to particular manufacturers. The instrument's make and model are usually printed on the headstock.

Strings

The thinnest string, which sounds the highest, is called the first string. The thickest, the sixth string, sounds the lowest. It's helpful to remember that the thinnest string has the thinnest number (1), and the thickest string has a thick number (6). On a four-string bass, the thickest string is the fourth string.

E, A, D, G, B, E

The six strings of a guitar (from thick to thin, low to high) are tuned to the notes E, A, D, G, B, E. These pitches can be easily memorized as Eating And Drinking Gives Brain Energy. A four-string bass has the strings E, A, D, G (one octave lower than the four thickest strings of a guitar).

Machine heads

Machine heads, which are also known as *tuners*, *tuning machines*, *tuning heads* and *tuning keys* are the metal devices on the headstock that are used to tighten and loosen

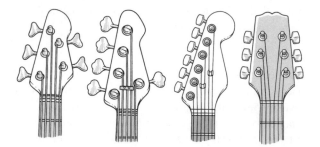

Different machine head arrangements – two five-string basses (left) and two guitars (right).

the strings. The section of the machine head that the string is actually wound around is the *post*, or *string post*. There are many ways of arranging machine heads on the headstock.

The nut
The strings run from the machine heads through the grooves in the *nut*. This little (usually plastic) strip holds the strings at the right height above the fretboard and the right distance from each other.

String trees
Some guitars have one or more *string trees* or *string guides* to stop the thinner strings from popping out of the grooves in the nut.

The bridge and saddles
The *saddles*, which sit on the *bridge*, hold the strings at the right height. On most solid-bodies the strings are also attached to the bridge, but on some there's a separate part for holding the strings, called the *tailpiece* or *string holder*. A guitar's *scale,* or *speaking length*, is the distance from the nut to the saddles.

Controls
Most electric guitars have at least two *controls* or *knobs* – one for volume and one for tone. Some guitars have four or even more.

Pickups
Most electric guitars have two or three pickups – one near the bridge, one close to the neck and, sometimes, one in-between. Most basses have two.

Pickup selector
The *pickup selector* allows you to choose which of the guitar's pickups you want to use. Even if there are two identical pickups, the one near the bridge will produce a different sound to the one closer to the neck.

Balance
Instead of a pickup selector, many electric basses have either two volume controls or a volume control and a *balance*

HOLLOW-BODY GUITAR

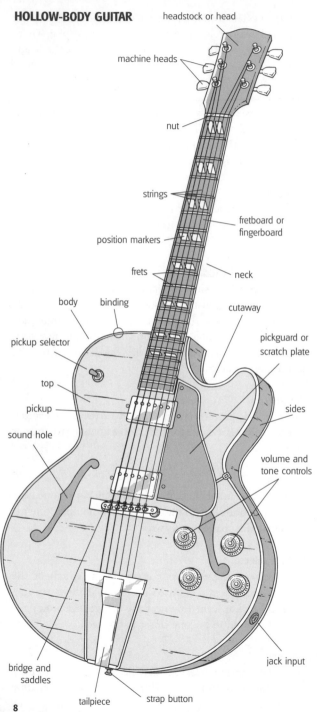

headstock or head

machine heads

nut

strings

position markers

frets

fretboard or fingerboard

neck

body

binding

cutaway

pickup selector

pickguard or scratch plate

top

pickup

sides

sound hole

volume and tone controls

bridge and saddles

tailpiece

strap button

jack input

control. These allow you to mix the sounds from the pick-ups or select each individually.

Tremolo arm
A *tremolo arm* (or *whammy bar*) allows you to bend notes up or down by making the strings tighter or looser whilst playing. The tremolo arm creates *vibrato* (if vibrated quickly), and *pitch-bend* (if used more slowly).

The jack input
The socket on a guitar for plugging in a lead is usually called the *jack input* (because it takes a cable with a *jack plug*). Technically, though, it's an output, since the signal comes out of, not into, the guitar.

THE HOLLOW-BODY
The name *hollow-body* refers to any electric guitar with a soundbox instead of a solid body. Hollow-bodies are rarely completely hollow, often having a beam inside to strengthen the structure and improve *sustain* (how long a note continues to ring after you play it).

The sound
Hollow-body guitars sound warmer, fuller, rounder and 'woodier' than solid-bodies. They give a slightly more 'acoustic sound', even when played through an amp. Hollow-bodies can be played without amplification, too, but most are not really designed for it and don't sound as good as real acoustics.

Jazz and thinlines guitar
Hollow-bodies come in a variety of shapes and sizes. Those with thick bodies (almost the size of acoustic guitars) are known as *jazz guitars* or *full-bodies*, and are mostly used by jazz players. Those with thinner bodies are known as *thin-lines*, *semi-acoustics* or *slimlines*, and are popular with blues, fusion and some pop players, as well as jazz musicians.

The top
A hollow-body's *top* or *face* is usually arched, which is why such guitars are also known as *archtops*. The top often has two *f*-shaped soundholes in it, just like a violin or cello.

9

Feedback

When playing at high volumes, guitars can create *feedback* – the high-pitched screech that is also produced by placing a microphone in front of a speaker. Feedback tends to be worse with hollow-bodies than solid-bodies; in general, the shallower the body, the less serious the feedback problem.

Binding

The *binding* is the decorative and protective strip that runs around the edge of a guitar's body (and neck and headstock on some models). Many solid-bodies also have binding.

LEFT-HANDED INSTRUMENTS

For left-handed musicians, there are special 'left-handed' instruments with everything fitted the other way around. However, left-handed instruments are less available and usually a bit more expensive.

Other solutions

Not all left-handers use a left-handed guitar. Many simply play right-handed, since the left hand is required to do just as much as the right hand. Jimmy Hendrix simply changed the order of the strings on a standard guitar and held it the other way around – the fact that this left his controls and tremolo arm in an awkward position never seemed to bother him.

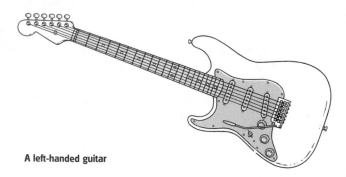

A left-handed guitar

3. LEARNING TO PLAY

Is it hard to play the guitar or bass? That depends on what you want to be able to do. You can learn the chords to a few tunes in just a couple of weeks, and picking up the bass parts may be even quicker. But you can go on learning forever. This chapter focuses on reading music, lessons and practicing.

One nice thing about the guitar and bass is that you can make music with just a few simple techniques. Many famous songs – from the blues to the Beatles and from metal to Madonna – use just a few chords or bass notes.

GUITAR AND BASS MUSIC ON PAPER

There are many ways to write music down and although many players don't 'read music' in the traditional sense, most guitarists can read chords, and most bassists can use them to find the right bass notes. The three most important ways of putting guitar and bass music on paper are introduced below.

Chord diagrams

Chord diagrams, or *chord charts*, are found in nearly all song books. They're easy to learn and can help you master thousands of tunes very quickly. They are simple diagrams that show you which fingers need to stop which strings at which fret. Any chord can be written down in a chord chart. See overpage for the basics of how these work.

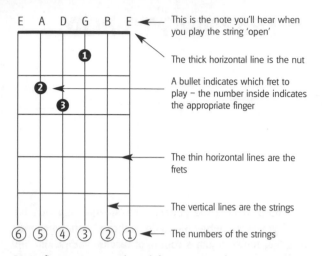

Your fingers are numbered from 1 to 4, from your index finger to your little finger. So, the above example tells you to play string 3 at the first fret with your index finger, string 5 at the second fret with your middle finger, and string 4 at the second fret with your ring finger. The result is an E major chord.

Play some blues

To play some blues, all you need is these three simple chords:

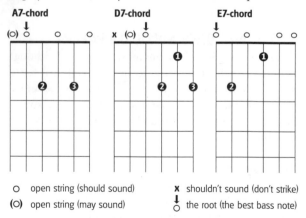

○ open string (should sound)	✗ shouldn't sound (don't strike)
(○) open string (may sound)	○̣ the root (the best bass note)

Play them in this order: 4xA7 2xD7 2xA7 1xE7 1xD7 1xA7 1xE7. Repeat this until you want to finish, but on the last time you play the sequence, change the last chord to an A7 (so then you play 4xA7 2xD7 2xA7 1xE7 1xD7 2xA7). This is called '12-bar blues'.

Chord books and cards

There are books available that list and name lots of chords in charts – like chord dictionaries. These can be helpful for using song books that list the chords by name but don't give charts. You can also get an electronic device no bigger than a credit card that stores hundreds of chord charts.

Tablature

There's also a system for writing down guitar and bass parts of all types – not just chords. It's called *tablature*, or *tab*, and most music shops have books that use the system. In most cases the music is also written out in regular notation (musical notes on staves) to indicate the exact rhythm, something tab doesn't show. If you know how the tune should sound, though, you'll usually be able to just read the tab line. The tablature staff represents a guitar neck. Here's how the system works:

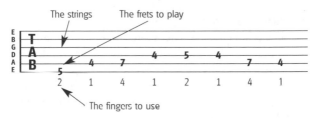

The six horizontal lines represent the six strings, and the numbers on the lines tell you which frets to play. If there are also numbers underneath the lines, they tell you which finger you should use to fret each note. Try playing the above example – if you repeat it you should get a boogie-woogie bass line.

Reading music

It's possible to play perfectly well, and to be a successful performer, without ever learning to read traditional music notation. Indeed, most famous rock guitarists can only read chords, and perhaps a bit of tab. However, being able to read music has many advantages – here are a few:

- You'll be able to use **thousands more music books**.
- You'll gain **a deeper understanding** of how chords – and entire songs – are structured.
- You'll be able to **write down** what you've played, or what you want someone else to play.

- It will make you more of an **all-round musician** – you'll be able to read and play parts that were meant for other instruments.
- And finally: learning to read music **isn't that hard at all**.

LESSONS

Thousands of guitarists and bassists, including plenty of famous ones, have never had a lesson, but consulting a teacher isn't such a bad idea. You could consider getting a few lessons, just to cover the basics, so that at least you start out the right way.

Not just notes

A good teacher won't only help you play the right notes, but also how to hold your instrument properly, read music, improvise, tune up and play different styles.

Questions, questions

Before deciding on a teacher there are some questions you may want to ask – and not only how much the lessons cost. Here are a few:

- Do you get a **free introductory lesson?** This is a good way to find out how well you get on with the teacher, and, for that matter, with the instrument.
- Is the teacher interested in taking you on as a student if you're just doing it **for the fun of it**, or are you expected to practice for hours every day?
- Do you have to make a large investment in method books right away, or is **course material provided**?
- Can you **record your lessons**, so you can listen at home to how you sound and to what's been said?
- Are you allowed to fully concentrate on **the style of music you want to play**, or will you be required to learn other styles?
- Is this teacher going to make you **practice scales** for a long time, or will you start straight off on pieces.
- Can the teacher **offer advice** on purchasing an instrument and other gear?

Finding a teacher

Music shops often have private teachers on staff, or they can refer you to one. You could also ask your local

Musician's Union, or a music teacher at a high school or music college in your area. If you see a good local band performing, try asking the players if they take pupils. Also check the classified ads in newspapers, music magazines and supermarket bulletin boards, and try the *Yellow Pages*.

Group or individual tuition?
Although most guitar students take individual lessons, you could also opt for group tuition, if it's available in your area. Personal tuition is more expensive, but it can be tailored exactly to your needs. Professional teachers usually charge around £15–30/$20–50 per hour for individual lessons.

Collectives and music schools
You may also want to check whether there are any teacher's collectives or music schools in your vicinity. These may offer you ensemble playing, masterclasses and clinics as well as normal lessons, and are sometimes considerably cheaper than individual tuition.

Get to work
Finally, visit festivals, concerts and sessions. Watch and listen to lots of bands and soloists. After all, seeing other musicians at work is one of the best ways to pick up tricks. Living legends or local amateurs – every gig's a learning experience. But the best way to learn to play? Practice.

PRACTICING
You can play without reading music. You can learn without a teacher. But there's no substitute for practice – here are some tips.

How long?
How long you need to practice for depends on what it is you want to achieve. Some top musicians have practiced eight hours a day for several years, or even more. And the more time you spend, the faster you learn. Still, just half an hour a day should ensure steady progress.

Keep at it
At first, playing can be quite uncomfortable, especially for your left hand, which does a lot of work in what initially

seems like a very awkward position. Also, the strings cut into your fingertips (on guitar) or give you blisters (on bass). Keep at it – your hand will soon get used to the position, and fingertips quickly develop hardened skin (*calluses*).

Volume

You don't always have to make lots of noise with your guitar or bass, and there's plenty you can practice without even using an amplifier. Also, many amps have a headphone socket, so you can play away all night without disturbing anyone. You can even get special practice amps that are only designed for using with headphones – they are usually about the size of a personal stereo and many come with built-in effects. Some even have a cassette player so you can play along with bands or backing tapes.

Practice rooms

Practicing with a band is not only loud, but requires lots of space, and often the best option is to rent a practice room. As well as giving you a place to play, practice rooms often have a drum kit and amps ready for use, so all you need to bring along is your instrument. Prices depend on the area, the size of the room and the equipment provided.

Protect your ears

Ears are very delicate, and high volumes can easily cause permanent damage. So if you want to play really loudly, a pair of earplugs or ear protectors is a good idea – in the practice room and on stage.

Earplugs

Earplugs are available from many music and hardware stores, in a wide variety of types and prices. The cheapest foam-plastic ones can make the other band members sound like they're in another room. Slightly more expensive are plastic earplugs, which vary greatly in their sound-reducing effect. The most expensive ones are custom made; they come with individually adjustable filters, which reduce the volume without changing the balance or the character of the sound.

Books, videos and CDs

Guitarists and bassists have endless practice material

available to them. Most music shops have a good range, but also try checking your local library:

- There are **song books and method books** available for every style of music, from those for absolute beginners to those for seasoned pros. Many of them come with tapes or CDs of examples and play-along exercises, which often provide a backing band and let you play the tune or solo.
- Lots of well-known players have made **tutor videos**. These video lessons usually last between thirty and ninety minutes, and sometimes come with transcriptions of the exercises.
- There are **CD-ROMs** that turn your computer into a guitar teacher – and there are even lessons available on the Internet.

Metronomes

In a band, the drummer plays the most important part in making sure the music doesn't speed up or slow down unintentionally. But all the members, especially the bassist, need to be able to keep a steady rhythm. That's why it's a good idea to practice, at least occasionally, with a metronome. It's a small device that ticks or beeps out a steady, adjustable pulse, helping you to work on your tempo, timing and rhythm skills.

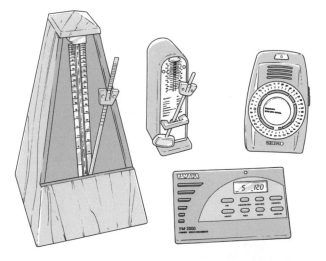

Two mechanical (clockwork) metronomes and two electronic ones

Electronics and computers

A drum machine is a great alternative to a metronome, giving you a whole drum pattern to play along to. And there are also machines, as well as software programs, that accompany you with bass lines, chords or even an entire electronic band. Phrase trainers are devices that can slow down a musical phrase from a CD, for example, so you can figure out even the meanest, fastest licks at your own tempo (you can also get software that does this).

4. BUYING A GUITAR OR BASS

One of the nice things about electric guitars and basses is that you can buy a decent one quite cheaply. You also need an amplifier, of course, but a small practice amp shouldn't set you back too much.

This chapter gives you general information about purchasing an instrument and chapters 5, 6 and 7 deal with the technical details.

You can buy a basic electric guitar for as little as £75/$100, and a small amplifier should cost about the same. You can, of course, spend twenty times that much – or more.

WHY PAY MORE?

Sometimes the differences between a cheap guitar or bass and an expensive one are not very obvious – so what exactly do you get for the extra money? First, better wood, and therefore a better sound. Second, a more expensive instrument often looks and feels better. Here are some other factors.

Hardware and electronics

Hardware is the name given to all the metal components and expensive instruments usually have better quality hardware – machine heads that will last longer, a bridge made of high-quality metal to bring out the best possible sound, good frets, and so on.

There are also differences in the quality of the electronic components. A quality pickup can cost as much as a beginner's guitar or bass.

Hand built

In the production of an expensive guitar or bass, more is done by hand and less by machine. Also, the quality control for high-budget instruments is usually much more thorough than for low-budget ones.

More options

If you buy an expensive guitar, you'll often have a number of options – a selection of woods, colours, finishes and pickups, for example. For some top-of-the-range models you can customize every last detail, and some players even have instruments built to their own design, but this doesn't come cheap.

Imitation

Many budget instruments look almost identical to higher-priced models. This is because designing a new type of guitar or bass is a time-consuming and costly business, and because people like to buy something that looks more expensive than it is. Just because it looks the same, though, doesn't mean that it will sound or feel as good.

Take a friend

You rarely find really bad guitars or basses these days, but they do exist. Instruments with warped necks, for example, or those that don't tune properly. If you haven't been playing for long, you might not be able to tell how good or bad an instrument is when you try it out, so if possible take someone along with a bit more experience – especially if you're looking at a secondhand instrument from a private seller. And before you buy anything, read Chapter 5, *A Good Instrument*.

Adjustments

No matter how good a guitar or bass, it will never play and sound its best until it has been properly adjusted, or *set up*. Factories often don't pay much attention to this, but good music shops do. You can find out more about having an instrument set up in Chapter 9, *Maintenance and Cleaning*.

PRICES

If you take the time to look around, you should be able to

find an instrument that feels and sounds reasonably good for around £150/$200. Instruments in this price range are usually considerably better than the least expensive models. A hollow-body of similar quality will cost you more, mainly because it's more expensive to make a soundbox than a solid body.

Now and then

Some of the most popular guitars and basses still look almost exactly like the first solid-bodies from the early 1950s, and the original instruments from that period are now valuable collector's items. They did make some superb instruments back then, but it's cheaper to buy a decent new instrument today than it was in the 1950s.

Exclusive instruments

Sometimes a guitar or bass is only very expensive because it's very rare, and not because it has a great sound. This is one reason why a more expensive instrument isn't always a better one.

Prices

Guitars vary in price depending on the country you buy them in. In the US guitars and basses are generally cheaper than in the UK, for example, and the difference is especially marked when it comes to American brands, such as Gibson and Fender. Also, different brands use terms like 'professional model' to mean instruments in greatly different price brackets. So, the following list is only intended to give you a rough idea:

Under £200/$250	Budget models
£200–400/$250–500	For beginners and advanced players
£400–800/$500–1000	Professional-quality instruments
£800–2000/$1000–2500	Top models
Over £2000/$2500	Exclusive models

Amps and effects

When you buy an electric guitar or bass you'll need an amp to go with it. And for some players effects pedals are also a must. Chapter 10, *Amps and Effects*, gives you lots of important buying tips.

SECONDHAND

A secondhand guitar or bass in good condition usually costs between half and two-thirds of its original price. And, just like with new instruments, those made by well-known brands sell for far more than equally good ones by lesser-known brands.

Shop or private sale?

1 Purchasing a used instrument privately – from an ad in the paper, for example – is usually cheaper than buying the same instrument from a shop. However, shops do have their advantages: you can go back if you have any questions or are missing a part, and you may well get a guarantee. Also, good dealers tend not to ask outrageous prices, whereas private sellers sometimes do – either because they don't know any better, or because they think you don't.

A wide selection

Another advantage of buying from a shop is that you get a wide selection. The more instruments there are in stock, the harder it will be to choose, but you'll be in a better position to compare specs, sounds and prices.

GETTING THE BEST

What really matters is choosing an instrument you feel comfortable with – in terms of sound, feel and looks. This is far more important than brand name, price, or technical details. If an instrument feels right, then you're likely to play better, at home and on stage.

The sound

It's good to have some idea of what kind of sound you want before you set out to buy an instrument. A good way to do this is to listen to the sounds that your favourite professionals create. If one player has a sound which you particularly like, try to find out what type of instrument they're using. Does it have single-coil pickups or humbuckers? Is it a solid-body or a hollow-body? Bear in mind, though, that much of a professional's sound is to do with the way they play, and the effects and amps they use. Also many top musicians play customized instruments that you won't find in a shop.

Shop around

It's best to shop around before buying an instrument. Get a feel for the range, prices and service each store offers. Also, talk to lots of salespeople as they all have their own 'sound' too.

MORE INFORMATION

If you want to know more, then get yourself stocked up with guitar magazines, which offer reviews of the latest gear. Also, pick up brochures and catalogues, although make sure you get the price lists to go with them, because as well as providing you with lots of information, they're designed to make you spend more than you meant to. The Internet is another good source for up-to-date product information, and of course there are loads of other guitar books too. More about these resources can be found on pages 110–111.

Trade fairs

One last tip: if there's a trade show or convention in your area, go along. You'll see all the latest gear, be able to try out loads of instruments, amps and effects equipment, and meet lots of other players – who are a great source of independent advice.

5. A GOOD INSTRUMENT

This chapter looks at the technical details of electric guitars and basses, such as the materials used and the frets, tremolos and electronics. With this information you're set to buy the best instrument possible.

Besides what an instrument looks like, which is purely a matter of taste, you'll choose a guitar or bass because it feels right, sounds good and works well. In the following pages, each of these three factors is dealt with in turn. Strings and pickups are so important that they are dealt with separately – in Chapters 6 and 7 – and amps and effects are covered in Chapter 10.

THE FEEL
Many things affect how a guitar or bass feels to play, such as the type of body, neck and fretboard, the way the instrument is set up, and the shape of the frets.

Balance
It's important to get an instrument that feels comfortable in all playing positions, so when you're testing out guitars or basses, try them out standing up as well as sitting down. One important factor is how they're balanced – an instrument with a heavy headstock and light body 'hangs' differently to one with a small headstock and heavy body. Sometimes you can improve the balance of a guitar or bass by moving the strap buttons a little.

The body

The shape and weight of the body are also important. Some people prefer a heavy, thick body, whilst others favour a light, small one. Most modern solid-bodies have rounded edges to stop the instrument digging into your chest, but some models, and most hollow-body guitars still have sharper edges.

The neck and fretboard

There are many types of necks and fretboards. What you'll find most comfortable depends mainly on the shape of your hands and fingers. Three important factors are:

- **Neck thickness.** For obvious reasons, players with big hands often prefer thicker necks.
- **Neck profile.** Some necks have quite flat backs, whilst others are more rounded (*U-neck*) or V-shaped (*V-neck*).
- **Fretboard width.** A wide fretboard means the strings are further apart. With solid-body guitars, the range of widths is not actually that big, most being just over 1.5" (4cm) at the nut and just over 2" (5cm) at the twelfth fret.

Radius

The fretboard of an electric body guitar or bass is usually curved, in the same way as a road, being slightly higher in the middle than at the edges. This curvature is called *radius* or *camber*. Radius is always given in inches, and the higher the figure, the flatter the fretboard. Most guitars have a radius of between ten and twelve inches, but some, such as those designed specifically for playing heavy metal, have a

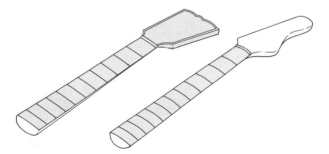

A thick neck with a wide, flat fingerboard (left) and a thin neck with a narrow, curved fingerboard (right).

radius of fifteen inches or more, which is very nearly flat. Hollow-bodies also tend to have almost, or even completely, flat fretboards.

Compound radius

With a very curved fretboard, when you bend a string it may rub against the higher frets. This is less of a problem on a fretboard with *compound radius*, which means there is more of a curve at the nut at the last fret.

A matter of taste

There's no 'best' type of neck or fretboard for any particular style of playing. Some guitarists find bending strings easier on a thick neck with a flat fretboard whilst others prefer a thin neck and a highly curved fretboard. And the same is true of playing chords.

Action

The term *action* refers to the distance between the strings and the fretboard – the higher the action, the bigger the distance. Action is the most important factor in determining how a guitar feels to play.

Set up

The action can be adjusted by altering – or 'setting up' – the saddles, nut and truss rod. This is important to bear in mind when you're testing guitars or basses, because if you find an instrument that sounds great but doesn't feel perfect, you may well be able to have it set up to suit you better. You'll find more on setting up guitars and basses in Chapter 9, *Maintenance and Cleaning*.

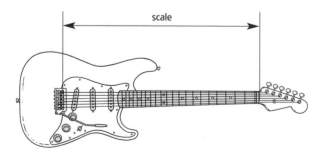

The scale is the distance between the saddles and the nut

Scale

The distance between the saddles and the nut – the section of the string that vibrates to create a note – is called the *scale*. Solid-body guitars usually have a scale of between 24 and 25 inches (61–63.5cm). The scale affects the way an instrument feels, and has a very subtle influence on the sound. Also, on an instrument with a short scale the frets are closer together, so you get a bigger difference in pitch when you bend a string.

Basses

Basses have longer scales than guitars, because their strings need to create much lower notes. Basses fall into three categories when it comes to scale, the most popular type being the *long-scale bass*, which has a scale of about 34" (86cm). These usually produce a deeper, fuller sound than *short-scale* basses, which have a scale of around 30" (76cm), although the latter type is easier to play if you have small hands. Between the two is the *medium-scale* bass, with a scale of roughly 32"(81cm).

Frets

How a guitar or bass plays also depends on the type of frets it has. Frets come in different heights, widths and shapes, from rounded to angular. You can even have the frets replaced, although this can be expensive.

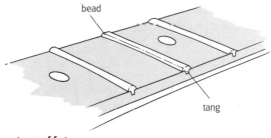

Three types of fret

Two octaves

Most solid-bodies have 22 or 24 frets, whilst hollow-bodies usually have 20 or 22. With 24 frets you can play two octaves on each string, because for each 12 frets that you go up the fretboard, the pitch raises by one octave. Basses usually have between 20 and 22 frets, but some have up to 26.

THE SOUND

Many things determine the sound of a guitar or bass – not just the strings and pickups. The wood used, the quality of hardware and the shape of the frets, for example, are all significant factors.

Unplugged

You don't have to amplify a guitar or bass to get an idea of its sound. Without amplification you can still hear whether an instrument sounds clear and bright, or warmer and more rounded. You can also hear how long the notes sustain for. Remember that the thicker strings should sound for slightly longer than the thinner ones, so if the B-string sustains longer than the D-string, something is wrong.

Amplified

So, it's a good idea to test an instrument unplugged first, but obviously you should never buy an electric guitar or bass without trying it through an amp. And when you do, always be sure to use a clean sound – at least for a while – since this will give you the best idea of the true character of the instrument.

The wood

Why does the wood of a solid-body guitar or bass affect the sound? Because the body and other wooden parts – as well as the nut, bridge, frets, etc – affect the way the strings vibrate. And it's these vibrations that are picked up by the pickups.

The body

The bodies of inexpensive 'solid-body guitars' are often made of chipboard, plywood or other non-solid wood-based materials. These usually produce shorter and shallower sounds than those made of two or more pieces of solid wood.

Different woods

The bodies of high-budget guitars and basses are made of woods such as basswood (linden), maple, mahogany, ash, poplar or alder. Naturally, each of those woods makes for a different type of tone and level of sustain. Mahogany bodies, for example, are often said to produce a warmer, fuller sound than maple bodies.

No two trees

No two trees are the same and there's high and low quality wood of any one kind. Bear this in mind when trying out instruments – just because a guitar has a body made of a particular type of wood doesn't mean that it will necessarily sound better than another.

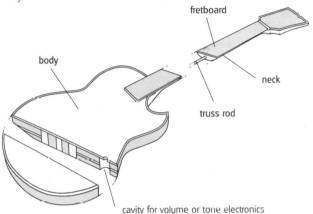

The wooden sections of a solid-body guitar

The top

Good-quality guitars often have bodies made of two pieces of wood that are the mirror image of each other (see Chapter 13, *How They're Made*). Sometimes a separate layer of wood is glued over the top of the body. This piece, called the *top*, is important to the way the instrument sounds, but also to how it looks, which is why an attractive type of wood is nearly always used. Maple is a popular choice, and bird's-eye maple is often used on high-budget models. Some inexpensive guitars have a synthetic top, made to look like wood.

Hollow-bodies

If you're buying a hollow-body guitar, you need to pay even more attention to how the instrument sounds unamplified, because the soundbox contributes greatly to the overall tone. Most important of all is the top, the part that the pickups are attached to, which is often made of spruce (like the top of a violin) or maple. Good quality hollow-bodies have a *solid top*, usually two pieces of solid wood glued together, while most inexpensive models have a *laminated top* (consisting of a number of thin wooden plys). Laminated tops tend to produce a shallower and less dynamic sound than solid tops.

Glue or screws?

The first solid-body guitars had the neck attached to the body with screws, not glue. This wasn't because of the sound, but simply because guitars were easier to build this way. Today, some guitars have glued necks and others have screwed necks; players often favour one type or the other, and most agree that a neck attached with screws produces a brighter sound. Yet again, though, there are no hard and fast rules, and you should buy an instrument because of its individual sound, not because it has a specific kind of neck.

Through-necks

On a guitar or bass with a *through-neck*, the neck and the central part of the body are made from a single piece of wood. So the body consists of a central strip with two 'wings' glued onto it. Through-necks are only found on high-budget instruments.

A six-string bass with through-neck

Fretboard

The fretboard is usually a thin piece of wood glued onto the neck, and the type of wood used affects the instrument's sound. A hard fretboard makes for a clear, bright tone, while a softer one produces a slightly rounder sound. Light-coloured maple and harder woods such as rosewood (brown) and ebony (even harder and nearly black) are often used.

Checking a neck

Always check that the wood grain of a neck runs straight (in the direction of the neck). The neck itself must also be straight, and not curved to the left or right. You can check this by looking down its length from the head. From here you should also be able to see whether the neck is twisted or warped at all.

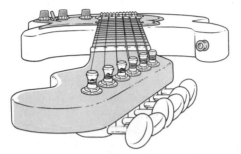

From this angle you can check whether a neck is warped or twisted

Out of line

You should also check that all the parts are in their proper places and correctly aligned. The picture below gives an example of a guitar with a badly placed bridge, resulting in the low E-string (number 6) lying too close to the edge of the fretboard. With this guitar, you'd probably keep pushing the string off the neck when playing in high positions.

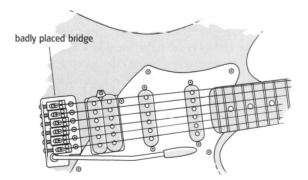

badly placed bridge

The thick E-string is too close to the edge of the neck and the thin E-string is too far away

Dead spots

The fretboard must be smooth and free from knots, cracks

and chips. If there are any knots, for example, they can result in *dead spots*, positions where the note produced sounds softer or doesn't sustain as long. It's important to check for these – even if the fretboard looks free from blemishes and knots – by playing each string at every fret.

The frets

The shape of the frets also affects the tone: narrower ones give a slightly sharper sound, and broader ones give a warmer sound. So-called *medium frets* are a little over 0.045" (1mm) high, and 0.090" (2mm) wide at the bottom. When testing an instrument, check that the frets are smooth and the right length. If they're too short, the strings may slip off them, if they're too long, they'll stick out from the edge of the fretboard.

Zero fret

A note played on an open string produces a different tone to a note played on a fretted string. This is because the nut, which the open strings run over, is wider than the frets, and made from a different material. To try and make open and fretted notes sound more similar, some guitars and basses have a *zero fret*, a fret right next to the nut. This way, the strings – open or fretted – always run over an identical piece of metal.

Fretless basses

An instrument without frets is harder to play in tune than a fretted instrument, because you have to stop the strings in exactly the right places, rather than just between two frets. Even so, *fretless bass guitars* do exist, and they're often said to have a more 'singing' tone. To make things easier for the player some have stripes where the frets would be, indicating where to stop the strings. Jaco Pastorius became world-famous with his fretless bass – he made his own instrument by simply pulling the frets off a standard bass and filling in the grooves.

The bridge and nut

Even small parts like the bridge and nut affect the sound. More expensive guitars and basses usually have heavy components – such as a sturdy, solid bridge – which give a broad tone and good sustain.

Every instrument

Professional guitarists and bassists often use more than one instrument during a gig. The bassist may use a fretless for just one song, for example, and the guitarist may swap between a solid-body and a hollow-body, or two solid-bodies with different sounds, or even two identical instruments with different tunings (see Chapter 8, *Tuning*). Some musicians have a few instruments on stage simply to avoid having to tune up, or in case they snap a string.

Active and passive

The sound of an instrument also depends on the type and quality of its pickups and electronics. Most guitars and basses have *passive electronics*, which means that the electrical signal goes from the pickups, via the tone and volume controls, straight to the amp. Guitars and basses with *active electronics* have a built-in *pre-amplifier* that boosts the signal before sending it to the amp.

The active sound

Put simply, all the tone controls do on an instrument with passive electronics is reduce certain frequencies. You create a treble sound by getting rid of the low frequencies and a bassier sound by taking away high frequencies. On an instrument with active electronics, though, the tone controls can actually boost frequency bands, giving you greater tone range and a little extra power. Guitars with active electronics, or *active guitars*, tend to be used by musicians who play very loudly, like heavy metal guitarists, but *active basses* are used in all kinds of styles.

Which is better?

Active electronics give you more options and power, but many guitarists and bassists prefer the sound of passive systems. Many bassists, for example, think that active electronics give too much of a neat, clean sound, although lots of active instruments have a switch for passive mode. Active guitars and basses usually start at around £400/$500.

Unplug the plug

A tip: unplug an active guitar or bass as soon as you stop playing. This switches the system off. If you don't, the battery that powers the pre-amp won't last very long.

Each is unique

No two guitars or basses have exactly the same sound – not even if they're the same make and series. So always play an instrument before you buy it, and don't simply take an 'identical' one from the storeroom.

THE MOVING PARTS

This section focuses on the moving parts: machine heads, tone controls, switches, saddles and tremolos.

Machine heads

Good machine heads work smoothly, making tuning easier. Most new guitars have *closed machine heads*, which have a metal housing over the cogs. The advantage of these is that no dust or dirt can get inside, and they're usually self-lubricating. Some guitars have *locking machine heads*, which allow for quicker changing of strings – you simply stick the string in the hole, lock the mechanism and tune up. However, it's sometimes said that they're less reliable than the traditional type.

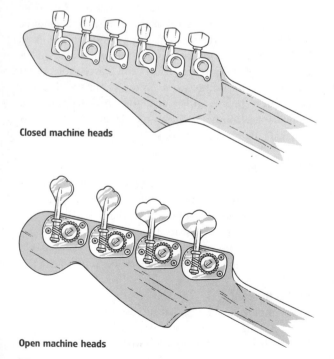

Closed machine heads

Open machine heads

Gear ratios

The *gear ratio* of a machine head affects the accuracy and speed of tuning. You need to turn a 10:1 machine head ten times to rotate the string post once; you need to turn a 14:1 machine head fourteen times to do the same. The higher the number the more accurately you can tune. If you like a guitar but don't like its machine heads, they can easily be swapped for better ones. And some manufacturers specialize in machine heads and other hardware (see Chapter 14, *Brands*).

Controls

The volume and tone controls on the guitar must be easy to use but still feel solid, and they should be placed for easy access during playing. Some controls click when they are in the middle position so you can feel where you are. Check whether the tone and volume controls work evenly – if you turn any knob gradually, the effect should be gradual.

Saddles

If a guitar sounds out of tune even after you've tuned it, or if you want to change the action, the saddles may have to be adjusted (see Chapter 9, *Maintenance and Cleaning*). On some bridges, the saddles sit in grooves to prevent them from moving sideways, which would alter the string spacing. Occasionally, the string spacing itself can be adjusted.

Tremolo

The tremolo arm allows you to reduce and (sometimes) increase the tension of the strings, making any chord or

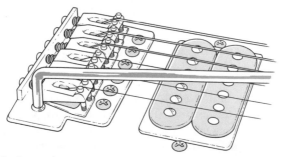

A basic tremolo system

note sound lower (or higher). It's a much-used tool, and can create anything from long, howling notes to fast vibrato. A set of springs makes the strings return to their original tension as soon as you let go of the arm.

Basic

One of the most basic tremolo systems is the Bigsby, which made its name on the older Gibson and Gretsch guitars. The world's most-used tremolo can be found on the Fender Stratocaster and the countless guitars based on its design. If you don't use your tremolo arm, you can take it off, or have the entire bridge fixed in place. You can also get *locking tremolos*, for instance those made by Wilkinson, which lock themselves when you aren't using them.

Floyd Rose

The American designer Floyd Rose gave his name to a tremolo system which could bend the notes much further (in both directions) than most previous systems. With a Floyd Rose tremolo, you can bend a note up to a high scream or down to the point that the strings become totally slack.

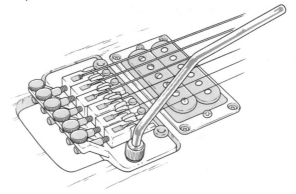

A Floyd Rose tremolo system with fine tuners (Jackson)

Locking nut

Floyd Rose also invented the *locking nut* or *top-lock*. This clamp, located just above the nut, locks the strings to stop them detuning when you use the tremolo arm. You tune up as normal and then tighten the nut to hold the strings in place.

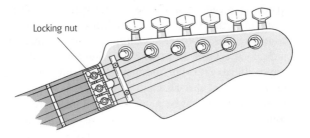

Locking nut

Fine tuners

Once the locking nut is tightened, you can no longer use your machine heads to tune. That's why guitars with a locking nut have *fine tuners* on the bridge, which allow you to adjust the tuning after tightening the nut. When using the fine tuners, don't put any pressure on the bridge, otherwise the tuning will change as soon as you let go. The best method is to listen, tune, let go of the bridge, listen again, and repeat until it's right.

With or without?

Floyd Rose-type tremolos are found on many types and makes of guitars, but not usually on those costing less than £250/$300. Some manufacturers allow you to choose whether you want a tremolo or not on certain models.

Checking a tremolo

When you're testing a guitar with a tremolo, it's worth considering a few points. Is the arm easy to use and remove? How much range does it provide? Does it cause the tuning to slip?

SECONDHAND

If you buy a secondhand instrument, there are a few things that need special attention.

- You may find an instrument with creaking machine heads. Sometimes this is just because it hasn't been played for a while, and can often be cured with a tiny **drop of oil**. New ones can be fitted if necessary.
- Examine the instrument for cracks, chips and other damage – especially on the **neck and fretboard** where a minor chip can make the instrument feel and sound noticeably worse.

- Listen out for unwanted noises such as **rattles or buzzes**. Sometimes these noises can be taken care of easily, by adjusting the action, for example, or tightening the pickguard screws. In other cases they can be almost impossible to get rid of and may require you to take the instrument to a specialist.

- If the instrument has been played a lot, it may have **worn frets**, with dents where the strings have been pressed to them. Worn frets can cause buzzing noises and make bending the strings difficult. Like all the other parts, frets can be replaced, but it's an expensive business.

- A **worn nut** can also cause unwanted noises. The nut can be replaced relatively cheaply.

- Finding the cause of a rattle or buzz is often harder than actually solving the problem. You can spend ages checking a whole instrument just to find that **one of the strings is loose**.

- Make sure all the **pickups** work. Connect the guitar or bass to an amp and press the strings down until they touch the pickups, one by one. You should hear a noise each time a string touches a pickup. Also, try playing with the pickup selector in all possible positions.

- Turn the instrument's **volume controls** up to full and down to nothing. Check that the change in volume is even. If you hear an high-pitched whistling when the controls are on full, there's probably something wrong with one of the pickups, and it will need to be replaced or repaired.

- **Take someone with you** who knows about guitars or basses, especially if you're going to look at a secondhand instrument from a newspaper ad.

6. STRINGS, PICKS AND LEADS

This chapter will help you choose the most appropriate strings, picks and leads (cords) from the bewildering variety of types and brands available. It also includes tips on fitting new strings.

The two or three thinnest strings of a guitar, known as the *plain strings*, are made of thin steel wire. The others, called *wound strings*, have a very thin metal wire wound around a central wire, and the material used for the winding affects the sound of the strings. Most players agree that steel windings give a clear, bright sound, that nickel windings give a warmer, less 'hard' sound, and that nickel-coated steel windings are somewhere in-between.

Heavy and light

When you buy a set of strings, you can choose between various *gauges* (thicknesses). The main differences between *heavy gauge* (thick) and *light gauge* (thin) strings are outlined below.

The differences between light and heavy gauge strings

Light strings	Heavy strings
• sound 'lighter' and sharper	• sound 'heavier' and broader
• don't sustain as long	• sustain for longer
• produce less volume	• produce more volume
• are easier to play	• make playing a bit heavier
• are easier to bend	• are harder to bend
• need to be tuned more often	• don't detune as fast
• break more easily	• last longer

Fractions of an inch

String gauges are given in fractions of an inch – a 010 string is 0.010 inches thick (one-hundredth of an inch, or 0.25mm). A set of strings is referred to by the gauge of the thinnest string, so a '010 set', or 'set of 10s', is a set with a 010 for the high E-string.

Names

Most manufacturers use names as well as numbers to indicate the gauges of their string sets. The following list gives the most common names, although some brands invent their own and the exact gauges of the other five strings in a 010 set, for example, vary from brand to brand.

Name of set	1st string	6th string
Extra Light/Ultra Light	008 (0.20mm)	038 (0.95mm)
Light	009	042
Regular	010	046
Medium	011	050
Heavy/Jazz	012 (0.30mm)	054 (1.35mm)

The most popular

The best-selling string sets for solid-body guitars are 010s and 009s. Solo rock guitarists usually favour light sets, blues and rhythm guitarists often go for 011s, and jazz guitarists tend to buy the heaviest strings. Some well-known brands are Dean Markley, GHS, D'Addario, Fender and Ernie Ball. D'Aquisto and La Bella are well known makes of jazz strings.

W

Thin sets usually have a plain third string (G), whereas thick sets tend to have a wound one. A wound third string is usually written with a W after its name, such as 020W.

Light top, heavy bottom

A guitar feels strange if it has one light string between two heavy strings. But some players do like to use light high strings, and heavier low ones. With this combination you can bend the top strings easily, but still produce a solid tone in the lower ranges. You can buy sets like this – they're usually called something like *Light Top, Heavy Bottom*.

Round-wound and flat-wound

Another option you have when choosing strings is whether to go for *round-wound* or *flat-wound*. Flat-wound strings are wound with a flat ribbon-like wire instead of a round one.

Round-wound and flat-wound strings

A round sound

Round-wounds are the most commonly used type of strings on electric guitars; they sound clearer and brighter, and often give a little more sustain. Flat-wounds sound slightly softer and more rounded, and make less noise when you slide your fingers along them. They're especially popular with jazz guitarists, and usually come in quite heavy gauge sets.

Ground-wounds

You can also get round-wounds that have been filed down to make them a little flatter. These strings are often called *ground-wounds* or *half-rounds*.

More tension

Heavy strings put more strain on an instrument than light ones. If you fit a guitar with much heavier or lighter strings than it had before, it's likely that the neck and tremolo will need some readjustment. Also, if the nut is designed for light strings, heavier ones may get stuck in the grooves, in which case you'll need to replace the nut or have the grooves widened.

Cheap or expensive?

A set of strings usually costs around £5–8/$6–10, although you can easily pay more. Bass strings are much more expensive, usually £15–30/$20–40 a set. Expensive strings tend to sound better and last longer.

String life expectancy

How long a set of strings lasts depends most of all on how much and how hard you play. Other important factors are the quality of the strings, how often you bend them and how often you clean them (see Chapter 9, *Maintenance and Cleaning*). People who get sweaty fingers when they play – especially if the sweat is acidic or alkaline – are likely to get through strings more quickly.

When to replace

As a guideline, you could try replacing your strings after about two or three months. If you can't hear any difference between the old and new strings, you've changed them too early, but if there's a marked difference you may want to change them sooner next time. Bassists tend to use the same strings for longer than guitarists.

One string or all?

Plain strings break more easily than the thicker, wound strings. And luckily you can get away with replacing one plain string without fitting a whole new set. If one of the wound strings breaks, though, it's best to replace them all (unless the set is quite new) because a new wound string will sound noticeably brighter than the older ones.

Bass strings

The strings of a bass need to be very thick in order to produce such low notes. Flat-wound bass strings were the most popular until the Sixties, but round-wounds have dominated the market since then. Many of the popular guitar string makers also produce bass strings, and some manufacturers, like DR, GHS and Rotosound, specialize in them.

Thick and thin

Bass strings also come in various gauges. Here are the most common types of sets:

Name of set	1st string (G)	6th string (E)
Extra Light/Ultra Light	030 (0.75mm)	090 (2.25mm)
Light	040	095
Medium	045	105
Heavy	050 (1.25mm)	110 (2.75mm)

MAKING STRINGS LAST

You can only get the best from your instrument if your strings are in good condition. Here are some tips on how to make strings sound as good as possible for as long as possible.

Sharp edges

To maximize the life of your strings, you need to take a close look at your guitar or bass. Sharp or rough edges can cause strings to wear out and break. If you keep snapping the same string in the same place, there's probably a chip or nick on your instrument.

Frets, nut and saddles

Rough frets contribute to string wear, but you can carefully smooth things down with some ultrafine steel wool (number 0000, sold in hardware stores). Sharp edges on the nut and saddle also cause strings to break prematurely. Again, some fine steel wool or ultrafine sandpaper will usually do the trick.

Dirt

Airborne dust and moisture, as well as dirt and grease from your fingers, cause strings to lose their brightness. Wound strings are especially sensitive to this, because particles settle in gaps between the windings. Generally, when strings start to look discoloured, they'll soon need replacing. They may not break for another year or two, or even more, but a new set will dramatically improve the sound.

Clean and dry

An easy way to keep your strings in good condition is to wash your hands and dry them well before playing, and to clean and dry the strings afterwards. Any lint-free cloth works well – an old T-shirt, for example. Wipe down the tops of the strings, but also pull the cloth between the strings and the fretboard, and run it up and down the neck a couple of times.

String cleansers

If you get very sweaty fingers, you may want to consider getting some special string cleanser, which removes the dirt from the grooves of your wound strings and also cleans the plain ones. It's not very expensive and a little bottle should last a long time.

Smoother strings
There are also products that are designed to make your strings feel smoother. They often help to repel dirt as well. There are various brands, such as *Finger-Ease* and *Fast Fret*.

Spare sets
Old strings are more likely to break than new ones, so the more often you change your strings, the less likely it is that you'll ever snap any. On the other hand, even a brand new string can break, so if you do a gig, be sure to have a spare set with you, or even a spare guitar.

Tuning
If you tune your strings too high, they may snap. Tuning to a tuning fork, an electronic tuner or a piano or keyboard will prevent this from happening (see Chapter 8, *Tuning*).

NEW STRINGS
Changing strings is easier with some tools at hand. First, a wire-cutter to cut the old strings. Second, a pair of pointed (*pincer-nosed*) pliers to help you get the ends of the old strings out of the machine heads without cutting your fingers. Third, a *string winder* to speed up the loosening and tightening of the strings.

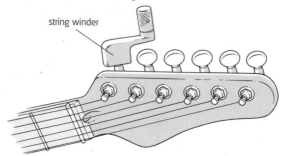

string winder

One by one
When putting on a new set, it's best to replace the strings one by one. If you remove them all at once, it will take the guitar some time to readjust to the tension when you fit

the new ones, and this will temporarily affect the tuning. Most guitarists start by changing either the low or high E.

Tuning as you go

Another advantage of changing the strings one by one is that you can tune each new string to the one next to it – assuming that the instrument is in tune in the first place.

Cleaning the fretboard

Some players like to remove all the strings at once, since it allows them to give the fretboard and body a good clean. There's an alternative way, though – simply replace the strings two at a time, cleaning underneath each pair as you go.

Elasticity

As strings lose their elasticity, they start to sound dull. The harder you play them, the faster this happens, but even if you fit a set of strings and leave them untouched, they'll sound dull eventually. When they're brand new, however, strings are far too elastic, and so when you put on a new set, you have to tune up again and again. Most strings don't sound their best until the tuning becomes a bit more stable; this usually takes a few hours.

Pre-stretching

A good way to get rid of the extra elasticity more quickly is to slide a finger along the underneath of the strings, one by one, whilst carefully pulling them upwards, away from the body – then retune. Repeat this process until the tuning becomes more stable.

On the table

You can change the strings with your guitar on your lap, but it's easier if you put it flat on a table. A towel or a piece of foam plastic underneath prevents scratches and keeps the guitar from sliding away.

FITTING STRINGS

If you fit new strings properly, they'll sound as good as possible and won't damage your guitar. There are several 'correct' ways to fit strings, one of which is described overpage.

Removing the old strings

Loosen, with a string winder if you have one, the first string (top E) or the sixth string (low E). When the string is totally slack, cut it in two places: near the bridge and near the machine head. This helps to prevent wear of the bridge and machine heads, as it saves you having to pull the whole string through them, and reduces the chance of

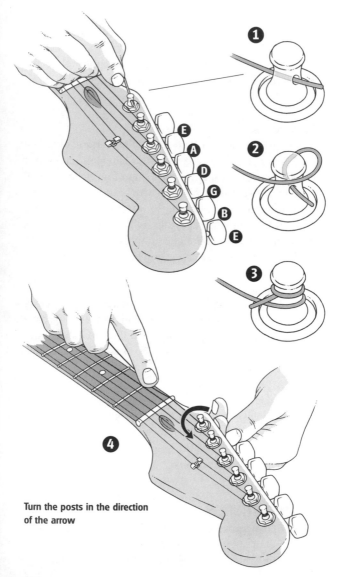

Turn the posts in the direction
of the arrow

scratching the paintwork when you remove the string. Make sure that the string has no tension left in it when you cut it, otherwise it can be dangerous for both you and your guitar. If necessary, use the pliers to carefully work the end of the string out of the machine head.

Fitting the new strings

Feed the new string through the hole in the bridge or body, and over its saddle. The ball at the end of the string keeps it in place. Here's what to do at the machine head:

1. Turn the machine head so that the hole faces the string, and feed the string through the post.
2. Pass the string over and round the post once.
3. Start winding the machine head, making sure that the string now runs underneath the end which is sticking out of the hole.
4. Lift the string from the fretboard with your other hand, keeping it under a little tension. Use your index finger to guide it through the groove in the nut.

Too long

Ideally, once the strings are tuned, the plain strings should be wrapped around the posts about four times; three is fine for the wound strings. Most strings are longer than they need to be, so don't attach them to the posts at their very ends or you'll end up with too many windings. You can either cut them after they've been fitted, or beforehand, leaving about 2"(5cm) for the windings.

A better tone

String posts have an hourglass shape, so that they push the windings of each string together. If a string is the right length, then once it has been tuned the windings should be packed together around the 'waist' of the post only. Surprisingly, if this is the case, then you'll actually get a better tone and your strings won't go out of tune as quickly.

String tips

• Don't get any kinks in your strings, because they can easily result in breakage. There's one exception to this rule – some players use a pair of pliers to make a small kink at the end of each string (after they've cut it to the right length), so that it hooks around the post.

- It may be hard to tell an E-string from a B-string once they're both out of their packets – so don't unpack a string until you're ready to put it on.
- Some manufacturers print the names or the numbers of each string on its packet. Others only print the gauges, usually in both inches and millimetres.
- Don't tune too high or too low. Tuning too high can damage your guitar and cause strings to snap; tuning too low can cause the strings to rattle against the frets. Besides, a guitar sounds best when it's tuned to the proper pitch. You can read more about tuning in Chapter 8.

Floyd Rose
On a guitar with a Floyd Rose tremolo (or one of the many of similar designs), the strings are attached to the bridge in a different way. You cut the ball-ends off, and the strings are held in place by small clamps, which you loosen and tighten with the appropriate tool – almost always an Allen key. When all the strings are fitted, stretch (see page 45) and retune them until the tuning becomes stable, and only then lock the strings at the nut. From then on you can't use the machine heads, and all tuning should be done with the fine-tuners at the bridge. If you do open the locking nut to use the machine heads, there's a risk that the strings will snap where they've been gripped.

Other brands
With some types of tremolo you have to fix the strings in a different way. Check your manual for guidelines, or ask in a guitar shop.

Different machine heads
Machine heads vary too. Some have the hole running lengthwise down the middle of the post, for example, or locking machines that help you put strings on really fast (see page 34). If you're changing the strings of a guitar for the first time, look how the old strings are attached before you replace them.

String trees
If there are string trees on your guitar's head, make sure the strings run under them, as shown in the picture opposite.

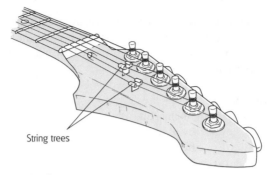

String trees

Hollow-bodies

On hollow-bodies, the strings are usually attached to a special string holder or tailpiece. In this case, too, it's best to replace the strings one by one, since if you remove them all at once, the tailpiece may come loose and scratch the varnish. Putting a cloth between the tailpiece and the body is a good way to prevent this.

The bridge

The bridge on some hollow-bodies is not glued or screwed down, but kept in place by the pressure of the strings. The position of the bridge has to be right, otherwise an octave on your guitar won't really be an octave (see page 72), and the tone will be altered. Changing the strings one by one will prevent the bridge moving.

PICKS

Most music shops offer a wide variety of *picks*, in all different shapes, weights, sizes and colours. Brightly coloured ones are easier to find if you drop them, but for the rest your choice depends on how you play, the sound you want, and what feels most comfortable.

Heavy and light

Each brand produces various weights of pick. A light one may be as thin as 1/64" (less than 0.5mm), but a heavy one can be more than twice as thick. Thicker picks make for a heavy, full-bodied sound – they both require and provide more precision.

Hard and soft

Generally, a thick pick is less bendy than a thin one.

However, different picks are made of different types of plastic, so you can get thick ones that are flexible and thin ones that are hard. If you want a really hard pick, try to find a metal one.

Which pick?

For chord playing many guitarists prefer quite thin picks, because they're easy to use and make for an even sound. Solo guitarists often go for smaller, harder ones, and players who get sweaty fingers often use a pick with a non-slip surface, or a rubber or cork grip. The only way to find out what suits you, though, is to try a selection – they're very cheap.

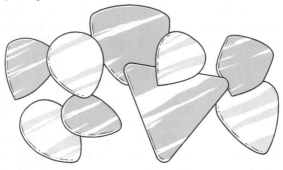

Picks come in many shapes, weights and sizes

Fingertips

Not all electric guitarists use picks. Playing with fingers and fingernails creates a much softer and rounder sound and allows you to play things that you couldn't with a pick. Country guitarists often alternate between picks and fingers.

Fingerpicks

For *fingerpicking* (a technique where you pluck a tune and chords with the fingers whilst playing a bass line with the thumb) many players use *fingerpicks* and a *thumbpick*. You slide one of these special picks onto each finger.

Bassists

Although most bassists play with their fingers, special bass picks do exist. They are bigger than guitar picks, and usually come in three thicknesses.

Brands

Well-known makes of picks include Dunlop, Fender, Gibson and Schaller.

LEADS

The leads used for connecting guitars and amps are called *jack leads*, because they have a jack plug on either end. If a lead is damaged (often the result of a wire in one of the plugs coming loose) you either hear nothing at all or humming and crackling. So however good your lead is, it's always worth having a spare – especially at a gig.

Good leads

You can get a lead for as little as £4/$6, although professional quality ones can cost £15/$20 or more. An expensive lead is not only more robust, but gives an audibly better sound (as long as the rest of your equipment is reasonably good). There are special leads for bass guitars that enhance the transmission of low frequencies.

Long leads

The longer a lead is, the higher the quality needs to be. If you have a good lead, a length of 15 or 20 feet (5–6m) is fine, but a cheap lead of the same length may give a less clear sound. If you have an instrument with active electronics (see page 33), the length of the lead has much less influence on the sound quality.

Cordless systems

If you have around £150/$200 or more to spare, you could consider getting a *cordless* system. They work just like cordless telephones, with a transmitter that beams a signal from the guitar to a receiver plugged into the amp. A cordless system buys you a lot of freedom on stage, but a good lead will generally give a sound which is just as good, if not better, for much less money.

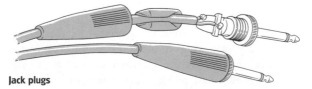

Jack plugs

7. PICKUPS

The magnetic pickups of an electric guitar or bass 'pick up' the vibrations of the strings and turn them into an electric signal, which is turned into sound at the amplifier and speaker. There are lots of types of pickups, each with its own sound.

On any stringed instrument, the section of a string near the bridge resonates with a much brighter, sharper tone than the rest of the string. You can test this out on an unamplified guitar – play the same string near the bridge and near the neck and listen to the difference in sound. Pickups recognize this difference, which is why most guitars have a *bridge pickup* (near the bridge) and a *neck pickup* (nearer the neck) allowing the player to choose between an incisive, penetrating sound and something more mellow. Some guitars have a third, a *middle pickup*.

TYPES OF PICKUP

A pickup basically consists of a magnet which has extremely thin copper wire wound around it several thousand times, turning it into a *coil*. There are *single-coil* and *double-coil pickups*, and you sometimes find both types on the same instrument.

Single-coils and humbuckers

Generally speaking, single-coils produce a clear, thin, sharp, trebly tone, whilst double-coils give more mid and low frequencies, producing a warmer, deeper, fatter, fuller sound. Double-coil pickups are often referred to as *humbuckers*, although technically the humbucker is a special type of double-coil (see page 57).

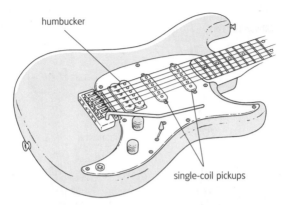

humbucker

single-coil pickups

A solid-body with two single-coil pickups and one humbucker

The humbucker range
There are many types of humbuckers, and they're capable of producing lots of different sounds – from powerful overdrive to a warm, broad tone. And that's why they're popular with metal guitarists and jazz players alike.

The single-coils range
There are also various types of single-coil pickups. One factor that varies is the amount of signal they supply to the amp. Strong pickups are good for overdriven, distorted sounds, and they make it possible to sustain notes for longer.

Strats and Les Pauls
The two best-known electric guitars are the Fender Stratocaster (the 'Strat') and the Gibson Les Paul. One of the main differences between these two models is that the standard Stratocaster has three single-coils, whilst the Les Paul has two humbuckers.

Listen first
When you go to buy your first guitar, it's a good idea to listen to a Stratocaster and a Les Paul (or similar models by other brands) first. Once you have heard the difference between these extremes, it will be easier to choose whether you want single-coils, humbuckers or both.

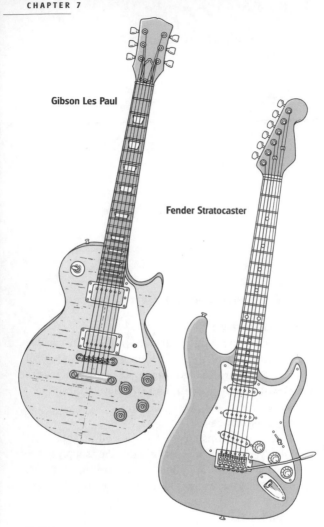

Gibson Les Paul

Fender Stratocaster

Coil-taps

Some guitars have a *coil-tap*, which is a switch that can make a humbucker work and sound like a single-coil pickup. Experimenting with an instrument like this is a good way to hear the difference between the two pickup types.

Changing pickups

If you're not happy with your guitar's sound, you might consider having your pickups replaced. It can cost a lot of money, though, to buy pickups and have someone fit them, so it's worth asking yourself whether your instrument is worth it.

BASS PICKUPS

There are single and double-coil pickups for basses too. Two types of single-coil are especially famous: the Precision (used for the Fender Precision bass) and the Jazz pickup (used on the Fender Jazz Bass). Similar designs are made by many other brands.

Both types

Many basses have both of these two pickup types. Usually the Precision-like model will be closer to the neck, allowing a thick, rocky sound, and the Jazz-type will be closer to the bridge, giving a more 'growling' sound and emphasizing mid-range frequencies.

Split pickups

Precision-type pickups are easy to recognize because they consist of two parts (which is why they're also called *split pickups*). The part under the thickest strings is usually closer to the neck than the part under the thinnest strings.

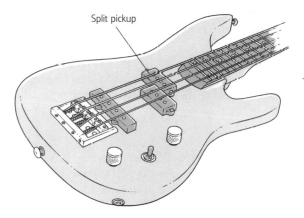

Split pickup

A split pickup consists of two parts

THE PICKUP SELECTOR

The pickup selector – or *pickup switch* or *toggle switch* – allows you to choose which pickup(s) to use. Guitars with two pickups have three-way selectors, whilst instruments with three pickups usually have five-way selectors, and the guitar sounds different in each setting. The diagram over-page explains the positions of a five-way selector.

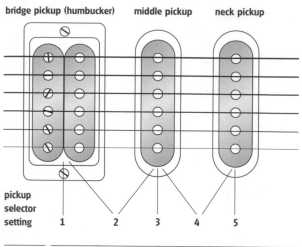

bridge pickup (humbucker)   middle pickup   neck pickup

pickup selector setting   1   2   3   4   5

setting	what you hear
1	only the bridge pickup
2	bridge pickup and middle pickup
3	only the middle pickup
4	middle pickup and neck pickup
5	only the neck pickup

Rhythm and lead

If a pickup selector can be switched from 'Rhythm' to 'Lead', the former refers to the neck pickup and the latter refers to bridge pickup.

Basses

Instead of a pickup selector, basses often have two volume controls (one for each pickup), or one volume control and a balance control. By adjusting these you can choose to use either pickup alone or a mixture of both.

HOW THEY WORK

The magnet in a pickup is surrounded by a magnetic field, which the strings run through. Because the strings are made of metal, when you cause them to vibrate they create a change in the magnetic field. This change is recognized by the pickup, turned into an electric signal and sent, via the volume and tone controls, to the amp. The fact that pickups respond to electromagnetic disturbances (instead of sound-waves like microphones) explains why an electric guitar wouldn't make any noise if you strung it with nylon, or any other non-metal, strings.

Reverse phase

The word humbucker comes from the fact that these pickups were designed to counteract humming noises: they 'buck the hum'. The two coils of a humbucker are in *reverse phase*, which means the magnets have been placed with their poles in opposite directions. If something causes one to hum, it will have the opposite effect on the other, and the two signals cancel each other out.

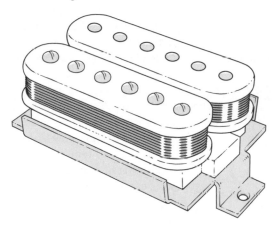

The two copper-wound magnets (coils) of a humbucker. This pickup can be adjusted for each string (see page 73).

8. TUNING

Each time you play a guitar, you have to tune up – or at least check the tuning. This isn't as hard as it may seem at first, though, you just need to know a few simple tricks, and learn how to listen in the right way. Read on...

When you first start playing, you're likely to find tuning easiest with an electronic tuner, but it's a good idea to know how to do it by ear – that way you can tune in any situation. The six strings of a guitar are tuned to the following notes:

String ①	**E** (the thinnest, highest-sounding string)
String ②	**B**
String ③	**G**
String ④	**D**
String ⑤	**A**
String ⑥	**E** (the thickest, lowest-sounding string)

Eating And Drinking

You can remember those notes with memory-joggers, such as Eating And Drinking Gives Brain Energy. The four strings of a bass are tuned to the same notes as the four thickest strings of a guitar (but one octave lower).

Playing on your own

When you play on your own, your strings have to be in tune with each other, but they

EADGBE
6 5 4 3 2 1

don't necessarily have to be exactly E, A, D, G, B and E. If they're a long way off, though, they can cause you a whole number of problems.

Too low, too high
If the overall tuning is too low, your guitar might still sound in tune, but the strings may rattle against the frets. Also, they'll be looser so you may accidentally bend them a little, causing you to play out of tune. If the strings are tuned too high, they're more likely to snap, the guitar will be harder to play and you may even bend the neck.

With a band
When playing with others, all the instruments must, of course, be in tune with each other. If you're playing with a piano, or any other instrument that cannot be tuned by the player, then you need to tune to that, but at other times you may have to tune to an electronic tuner, a metronome or a tuning fork.

Tuning to a keyboard
The diagram below shows you where the pitches of the open strings of a guitar and bass lie on the piano keyboard. You can tune each string to the relevant note one by one, but you should also know how to do *relative tuning*, which is explained overpage.

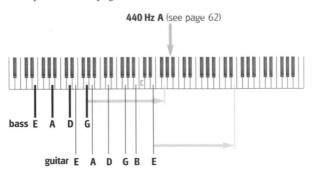

440 Hz A (see page 62)

bass E   A   D   G

guitar E   A   D   G   B   E

The four strings of an electric bass are tuned an octave lower than the four lowest strings on a guitar.

Tuning forks
A *tuning fork* is a small, two-pronged metal fork that produces a note for you to tune to. You tap it against your

knee and then either hold it near your ear or touch the base of it to the body of your instrument to hear the note. Most tuning forks produce the note A, because that's the note that most classical musicians tune to, but you can also get ones that produce the note of the guitar's open high E-string. The best way to tune to an 'A' tuning fork is discussed later in this chapter – for now, we'll concentrate on the E.

A tuning fork

RELATIVE TUNING

Once you have one string in tune, you can tune all the others from it – a process called relative tuning. It's possible to tune a guitar to any note, but it's easiest to tune to one of the notes of the open strings. If you're tuning to a piano, a keyboard, another guitar or an 'E' tuning fork, then you can tune your high E-string first. Here's what to do:

- Play your reference E (on the keyboard, tuning fork, etc) and listen to it for a few seconds.
- Play your open E-string, and try to hear whether the note sounds higher or lower.
- If the guitar's note sounds lower, tighten the string slightly.
- If the guitar's note sounds higher, first loosen the string until it sounds too low, and then slowly tighten it from there.
- Keep comparing and altering until the two notes sound exactly the same.

Singing

If you find it hard to hear whether the note of the guitar is higher or lower, try singing the notes as you play them – you'll soon learn to 'feel' the difference.

Fretboard diagrams

When a guitar is properly tuned, playing the B-string at the fifth fret creates the same note as playing the high E-string open. This is shown in the first fretboard diagram, and the similar relationships between the other strings are shown in the other four diagrams. Here's how they work:

- The numbers of the strings are shown at the bottom.
- The names of the strings are shown at the top.
- The black dot shows you where to fret the strings.
- The small circle underneath shows you which open string the fretted note should sound the same as.
- The letters at the very top show you which two strings each diagram deals with, and the note that you should hear when you're comparing them.

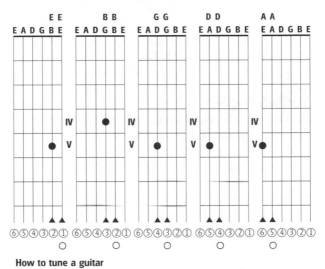

How to tune a guitar

Tuning the B to the E

Play the high E-string (that you just tuned) and listen to the note for a few seconds. Then play the B-string at the fifth fret, as shown on the diagram. If the B-string sounds too low, carefully tighten it. If it sounds too high, first loosen it until it sounds too low, and then slowly tighten it up from there.

And so on...

Now, continue to tune the other strings in the same way, as shown in the diagrams. Notice that you use the fifth fret (indicated by V) to tune all of the strings, except when you tuning the third one (G) to the second (B). Here, you use the fourth fret (indicated by IV).

The 440 Hz A

Sometimes you may have to tune with an A as your reference pitch, because it is a standard tuning note. The particular A that most musicians use is technically known as the '440 hertz A', because it is made up of exactly 440 vibrations per second. It is the note of most tuning forks, and lots of electronic metronomes can also produce it.

Tuning to the A

The 440 Hz A is two octaves higher than the guitar's open A-string. The best way to tune to it is to compare it with the fifth fret harmonic on the A-string (see the section on harmonics opposite). On a bass, its best to use the seventh fret harmonic on the D-string, although the A produced is still an octave lower than 440 Hz.

TUNING BASSES

Tuning a bass is essentially the same as tuning the four lowest strings on a guitar – you get one string right and tune the others from it. Some players tune the E or A strings first, but here we'll start with the G.

Tuning to a guitar

If you're tuning to a guitar, you can tune your first string (G) to the guitar's third string (G), but the notes are an octave apart. Some players prefer to tune using the twelfth fret

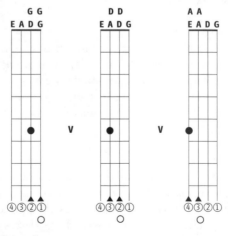

How to tune a bass

harmonic instead of the open string (see the section on harmonics below) because this way the two Gs are the same octave. If you want to tune to a piano or keyboard, see the diagram on page 59.

Tuning the other strings

Next, tune the D-string by playing it in the fifth position and comparing it to the open G. When it's in tune, compare the fretted A to the open D, and finally the fretted E to the open A. All this is shown in the diagrams opposite.

HARMONICS

Place a finger very softly on a guitar or bass string, exactly above the twelfth, seventh or fifth fret, and strike the string pretty hard and close to the bridge with your other hand. What you'll hear – with a little practice – is a high, thin tone known as a *harmonic* or *overtone*. Harmonics are often used by players for their specific sound, but are also very useful for tuning.

Why use harmonics?

Tuning with harmonics has numerous advantages. First, the note of a harmonic keeps on sounding even when you've removed your left hand from the string, so you can tune the note whilst actually listening to it. Second, there's a good method to help you hear when the strings are exactly in tune. When the two harmonics you're using to tune a string are almost the same and played simultaneously, you'll hear a wavy rhythm. When you do, carefully tighten or loosen the string that you're tuning. The closer you get, the slower the rhythm becomes. When the waves disappear, the two strings are in tune with each other. If the rhythm speeds up again, then you've gone too far.

Harmonics diagrams

These diagrams work in exactly the same way as those on page 61, except here the black dots indicate where you should lightly touch the strings to create harmonics. In all except one of the diagrams there are two harmonics, which you should tune to sound exactly the same. As the fourth diagram shows, when you come to tune the B-string, you have to play it open and compare it with the seventh fret harmonic of the low E-string. (You can use the twelfth fret harmonic of the B-string instead of playing it open but this raises the pitch by one octave.)

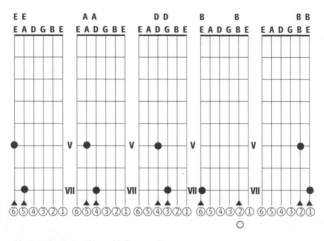

How to tune a guitar with harmonics

A trebly tone

You'll hear harmonics (and the wavy effect) best if you strike the strings near the bridge, use only your bridge pickup, and select a trebly sound on you guitar and amp tone controls.

TUNING TIPS

- Always tune a string by **increasing the tension**. If a string sounds too high, first loosen it until it sounds lower than it should be, and then tune it up from there. This way it's easier to hear what you're doing, and the strings keep their tuning better.
- A set of **pitch pipes** is a cheap, small alternative to a tuning fork or an electronic tuner. They have the advantage of giving you the note of each string, but they sometimes slip out of tune themselves, so a tuning fork is a better purchase.
- If your strings **go out of tune** quickly it could be due to many factors. It might be a simple problem, like worn strings (replace them) or slipping strings (attach them properly), or something more serious, such as faulty machine heads or a tremolo with weak springs.

- If **the nut's grooves** aren't wide enough for the strings you're using, tuning may be difficult and uneven. A temporary solution is to press the string behind the nut while you're tuning it (tune, press, listen, tune, press, etc). A better solution is to have the nut replaced or adjusted.
- Tuning can be made even smoother if you sprinkle some **graphite** (available at most hardware stores) into the grooves of the nut, or rub them with a pencil point.
- Instructional **videos and CD-ROMs** with play-along exercises often give you a note to tune to.

Intervals

An *interval* is the difference in pitch between two notes. Some players like to tune up by listening to the intervals between the strings, without fretting them or playing harmonics. The A-string is supposed to sound a *perfect fourth* (five semitones/half-steps) higher than the low E-string. A perfect fourth is what you hear when you sing the first two syllables of *Amazing Grace*, *Here Comes the Bride* or *Oh, Christmas Tree*. Sing the first syllable at the pitch the low E-string gives you, then tune the A-string to the pitch of the second syllable.

Oh When the Saints

The same interval is used when going from strings A to D, D to G, and B to high E. The only exception is going from G to B – the interval between these strings is a *major third* (four semitones/half-steps). When tuning the B to the G, you can use the first two syllables of *Oh When the Saints Go Marching In*.

ELECTRONIC TUNERS

Yet another way to tune your guitar is to use an *electronic tuner*, or *tuner*. These devices 'hear' the note you're playing, and tell you whether it's in tune, too high, or too low. On some models you have to set a dial to tell the tuner which string you're tuning. *Chromatic tuners*, which are usually more expensive, actually recognize the pitch you're playing and indicate it on the display. On both types, there are usually two arrows that tell you whether you should tune up or down to get the exact pitch.

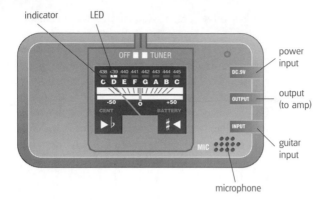

indicator   LED

power input

output (to amp)

guitar input

microphone

A chromatic electronic tuner indicates which tone it 'hears' (Seiko)

Bass tuners

Special bass tuners are available, but bassists can also use most guitar tuners. Some recognize the notes of the open strings of a bass, but others only work if you tune using the harmonics above the twelfth or fifth frets.

Tips

- A tuner allows you to tune **very quietly**, but also makes it possible to tune in a noisy environment, because you don't have to use your ears.
- After you've tuned with a tuner, it's a good idea to **check your tuning** with one of the relative tuning methods described on pages 60–62.
- If a sharp sign (♯) lights up on a **chromatic tuner**, it means you're playing a note that's one semitone/half-step higher than the name of the note indicated. For example, if a D and a ♯ light up, you're playing a D♯, and you need to tune down to get to a D.
- The flat sign (♭) indicates that a note is **one semitone/ half-step lower**.

OTHER TUNINGS

Some bands, such as Green Day and Offspring, tune their instruments a semitone/half-step lower than normal – E-flat, A-flat, and so on – to make their instruments sound a little fatter and the strings easier to bend. Also, the lower tension allows them to use slightly heavier strings, which give a thicker tone.

Capos

A *capo* is a special clamp that you attach to the neck of a guitar – just behind any fret – to change the overall pitch of the instrument. If you put it in the first position, all your strings sound a semitone/half-step higher; in the next position they sound a tone higher, and so on. Capos are especially useful for playing with singers (including yourself) because it makes it easier to sing songs which otherwise would be too high or too low.

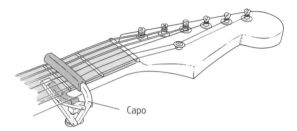

Capo

A capo in the second position – note that it is placed just next to the fret

Open tuning

There are various ways to tune a guitar other than E, A, D, G, B, E. The most popular alternative is to use an *open tuning*, which means the notes of the open strings form a particular chord. A common example is D, G, D, G, B, D (from low to high). This is known as *G major tuning* because strumming all the open strings together creates a G major chord (a chord made up of the notes G, B and D). With an open tuning you can play many chords, and often whole songs, just by placing your left-hand index finger over all six strings and sliding it from fret to fret.

Slides

Open tunings work particularly well with a *slide*. A slide is a tube, usually made out of metal, which you put on one of your left-hand fingers and 'slide' over the strings. They are especially popular with country and blues players. The term *bottleneck* is also used, because the first slide players actually used the necks of bottles – and glass slides are still available today.

More tunings

G major tuning is often used by fingerpickers as well as

slide players. Fingerpickers also favour D, A, D, G, A, D (known as 'Dadgad' or *D tuning*), which was first used by English folk guitarists. Some players use their own personal tunings. For example, E, A, C♯, E, A, E (*A major tuning*) was made famous by Bonnie Raitt. And King Crimson's Robert Fripp developed the C, G, D, A, E, G tuning, although he kept it secret for a long time.

D-tuner

Its sometimes useful to tune your low-E string down to D, but this is a problem if you have a guitar with a locking nut, since the fine tuners won't tune the string that low. However, you can get a device called a *D-tuner*, which takes the sixth string between E and D at the touch of a button.

9. MAINTENANCE AND CLEANING

This chapter tells you the basics about setting up the action and intonation of a guitar or bass – although most adjustments are best left to an expert. You'll also find tips on interference, cleaning, cases and insurance.

A guitar or bass only plays really well if it's properly set up. Some of the important adjustable components are the saddles, the neck and the nut, and these are the parts that determine the action (the height of the strings above the fretboard).

ACTION

Action is a matter of preference – some players like quite a high action, whilst others prefer the strings much lower. However, the action can be too high or too low. sIf it's too high, you have to press the strings very hard, especially in the highest positions (close to the guitar's body), making playing unnecessarily difficult. And if the action's too low, the strings may rattle and the sound may be poorer.

High and low

A guitar with a 'low action' will generally have a distance between the twelfth fret and the underside of the top E-string is less than about 0.50" (1.3mm). A distance of 0.90" or more is usually described as a high action. On a bass the action is usually between 0.90" and 1.20" (2–3mm), again measured at the twelfth fret.

Who uses which?

If you tend to strike the strings pretty hard or if you mainly play chords, you'll probably prefer quite a high action. Solo guitarists often prefer a lower action, because it makes fast licks and string bending easier. Bass players choose a high or low set up depending on the techniques they use.

The nut

If you're not happy with the action of your instrument, don't immediately start adjusting the saddles and neck. First have an expert check whether the height of the nut is right for the action you want.

The saddles

The height of the saddles can usually be adjusted. Many guitars and most basses have one saddle per string; others come with one for every two strings. Some players prefer to set the middle strings a little higher than the outer strings, so they follow the radius of the fretboard (see page 25–26).

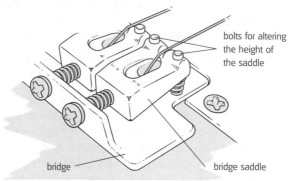

bolts for altering the height of the saddle

bridge

bridge saddle

On a bridge like this each string can be raised or lowered individually

The whole bridge

On many hollow-body guitars, and some solid-bodies, you can move the whole bridge up or down at once. Remember to loosen the strings first.

Resetting

If you adjust the saddles or the bridge it's useful to make a note of how many times you've turned each bolt. This will make it easier if you want to reset everything to the original position.

THE NECK

The neck of a guitar or bass should be very slightly concave – dipping a little between the headstock and the body. To check this, fret the bottom E at both the first and the fifteenth positions. With the string held down at these two points you should be able to see a small gap between the strings and the frets in the middle of the neck. If you can't, the neck is flat, or even a convex, which may mean the strings will rattle against the frets. If there's more than about 0.45" (1mm) between the string and the frets, the neck is too concave, which will make the instrument harder to play.

A third hand

If you can't see whether the string is touching the frets or not, get someone else to pluck it in-between your two hands. If the string sounds, the neck must be slightly concave, which is exactly what you want.

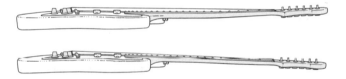

An overly concave neck (top) and an overly convex neck (below)

Neck first

There's little point setting up the saddles if the neck hasn't been properly adjusted, and this is a job for an experienced repairer. If you insist on doing it yourself, never give the truss rod adjustment bolt more than one complete turn in either direction. If it needs more than that it should really be done by a specialist.

Strings and action

If you change to much heavier or lighter strings than were previously fitted, the neck may well need to be adjusted. Heavier strings put more tension on the neck, making the action higher, and lighter strings, obviously, do the opposite.

Strings and tremolo

Changing string gauges can also affect the tremolo, which

works with a set of springs. Heavier strings put more tension on these springs, and lighter strings put less, so an adjustment may be necessary.

INTONATION

If the *intonation* of a guitar or bass is not correctly set up, the notes played on the higher frets are slightly out of tune with those played on the lower frets. If the intonation is right, a string played at the twelfth fret should sound exactly one octave higher than when it's played open.

Check

You can check the intonation of each string by comparing the note you get by fretting the string at the twelfth position with the harmonic above the twelfth fret. The two pitches should be identical – if they're not the intonation needs to be adjusted. This requires some very careful listening, and an electronic tuner may help.

Higher or lower

If the harmonic sounds higher than the fretted note, the section of the string that vibrates to make the note – the bit between the nut and the saddle – is too short. You can solve this by turning the saddle's screw so that it moves backwards slightly. This increases the string's speaking length. If the harmonic sounds too low, you need to move the saddle slightly forwards, towards the neck, making the *speaking length* of the string slightly shorter.

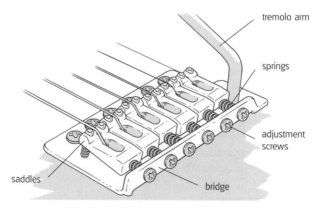

tremolo arm

springs

adjustment screws

saddles

bridge

Turning the screws adjusts the intonation

THE PICKUPS

The height of the pickups is also adjustable. The closer they are to the strings, the louder a guitar or bass sounds. Some pickups can even be altered for each string individually. Pickup adjustments, too, are best done by an expert.

Stratitis

If the pickups are set too high, the strings might rattle against them. Also, you may find that some of the notes – especially those played on the wound strings in high positions – sound slightly out of tune. This effect, which is caused by the magnets pulling the strings towards them, is most problematic on guitars with single-coil pickups. It's known as *stratitis* or *string-pull*.

CLEANING

A clean guitar or bass plays better, looks better and sells better. Every player has their own cleaning techniques, but here are a few good tips.

Clean strings

Clean strings sound clearer, last longer and don't make your fretboard and frets dirty. The easiest way to keep them clean is to regularly run a lint-free cloth over and under them – and the result will be even better if you moisten the cloth with a little *rubbing alcohol* or a special *string cleaner*. Be careful never to spill any of these liquids on the instrument, as they could damage the finish. Some guitarists carefully flick their wound strings against the fretboard a couple of times after playing, to get rid of sweat and dirt.

Boiling bass strings

One way to make bass strings last a bit longer is to boil them. Simply put all the strings in a pan of boiling water for a few minutes – some people add vinegar, soda, detergent or dishwashing liquid – and then rinse them well with cold water. Dry them carefully to prevent rust, removing any remaining dirt at the same time.

Breakage

Strings that have been boiled are more likely to break, not because of the boiling itself but because they've been fitted twice. Many bassists swear by boiling strings, whilst others think it's a pointless exercise. Either way, once a set has been boiled once or twice, boiling them again won't really make much difference.

The fretboard

Running a dry, lint-free cloth under the strings also cleans the fretboard and the frets. And an old, fairly soft toothbrush is useful for cleaning down the edges of the frets and the nut. There are special cleaners available for unvarnished fretboards, often with names like *fingerboard oil*; some players even use cooking oils (olive, peanut, etc) but the chances are that these will only make your fretboard greasy. You should never use any kind of oil on a varnished fretboard.

The body

What you should use to clean the body of your guitar or bass depends partly on the type of finish it has. Most varnished bodies can be easily cleaned with a very slightly damp cloth, or with one of the many special guitar cleaners available (*guitar polish*, *guitar juice*, *guitar gloss*, etc). Some of these products are only meant for cleaning the woodwork, whilst others are also supposed to restore the original lustre. Always read the instructions before choosing and applying any guitar cleaner because what's good for one finish can actually damage another. Certain bodies, such as those finished with oil or wax, require specific types of cleaners.

Furniture polish

Some guitarists, including experienced ones, happily use household furniture polish on their instruments. However, others warn against it, claiming that these products can cause the build-up of a greasy residue on the instrument's surface. Special guitar cleaners, at least theoretically, don't have this effect. Guitar cleaners do cost more, but they last a long time, so in the long run you may not actually save that much by using household products.

When in doubt

If you're not sure what to use on your instrument, take it to a guitar shop or repairer and ask for advice – and never use anything abrasive.

Brands

Guitar cleaners are supplied by many companies, including D'Andrea, Dunlop, Number One, GHS and Kyser. Some guitar manufacturers also make their own cleaners.

INTERFERENCE

Almost all guitars and basses buzz, hum or hiss to some extent, but there shouldn't be too much unwanted noise. If there is, the interference might be caused by your cable, instrument or amplifier. It could also be the result, though, of endless other things, such as a nearby fluorescent light or train track.

Leads

Most often, your lead will be the culprit. Sometimes simply pulling the plug out and then plugging it back in may help, but only temporarily. The easiest way to test the lead is by trying another in its place. Likewise, you can check the guitar by trying a different guitar through the same lead and amp.

Plugs and sockets

Sometimes you can stop background noises by using a different mains socket. If you live near a power station, train track, or other high-voltage cables, then special suppression equipment – sometimes available at music stores – may help.

A noisy instrument

Buzzing from your instrument may be caused by bad connections between the pickups and the controls or by poorly isolated pickups and wiring. Single-coils tend to cause more buzzing than humbuckers. If you can't locate or sort out the problem, ask music shop staff or a repairer for advice. If you use a distortion pedal, remember that it amplifies everything, including things you'd prefer not to hear.

ON THE ROAD

If you're taking your guitar or bass on the road, you should be extra careful. Here are a few tips.

Cases and covers

If you want your instrument to stay in good condition, it should have some kind of case. You can pick up a soft cover with no padding for as little as £7/$10, but at this price it will probably offer very little protection.

Gig bags

Gig bags are soft cases with a protective inner lining. They cost around £15–35/$25–50, depending on the level of protection they provide. Most come with either one or two adjustable shoulder straps, and some have outside pockets, which are handy for stashing strings, picks, etc. If you're buying a gig bag, make sure that the zip is sturdy and well covered on the inside, so that it doesn't scratch your instrument.

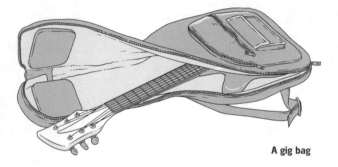

A gig bag

Hard cases

Hard cases, or *hard-shell cases*, are more expensive and heavier to carry around than gig bags, but they offer much better protection. A good hard case is sturdy and well padded, but it's also important to get one that perfectly fits your guitar or bass. A case that's the wrong shape inside can result in such serious damage as a bent neck. Many guitar cases come in a shape that closely follows the outline of the instrument. These don't offer as much space for accessories as rectangular ones but they take up a little less room.

Temperature

Sudden changes in temperature are bad for musical instruments. So if you come into a warm house from a cold street, for example, it doesn't do any harm to leave your instrument in its case for a little while, to let it adjust to the temperature slowly.

Humidity

Dry air is also bad for a guitar or bass, and if the wood gets too dry it might contract or even split. Dampness isn't good either – it mainly affects the strings and other metal parts, including the electronics.

Hygrometer

Central heating and air conditioning both cause dry air, but if a room doesn't feel too dry for you, then its probably not too bad for your instrument, because people and guitars like about the same level of humidity – around 50–60%. You can measure humidity with a *hygrometer*, which is available for as little as £15/$20 from most hardware stores. Digital versions are more accurate and reliable, but they start at about twice that price.

Serial numbers

Check whether there are serial numbers on your instrument, amplifier and other equipment, and make a note of any you find (there's a form to do this on page 112). If your gear gets stolen or lost, police and insurance companies may want these numbers.

Insurance

If you have home contents insurance, it may cover your guitar or bass (if it's not worth much) against theft from, or damage due to fire in, the home. However, musical instruments usually fall under the 'valuables' insurance category, which means that you have to notify the company when you buy or acquire a guitar, and sometimes have to pay more. If you want your guitar to be covered against accidental damage, or when it isn't in the home, you usually have to extend your policy – and this is sometimes surprisingly expensive. Another option is to take out a totally separate policy for your instrument and equipment.

Spares

It's a good idea, especially of you're doing a gig, to have certain spares with you: a lead, a set of strings, picks, and batteries for effect pedals and active electronics. And keep any tools you may need in your case, such as the Allen key for the locking nut, if you have one.

Stand

A guitar stand is handy for when you take a break from playing, or if you want to use more than one guitar or bass in a gig. There are a wide variety of models available, some of which are specifically designed to fold away very small, and others that are designed more for sturdiness.

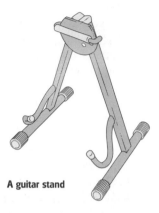

A guitar stand

Cars

Try not to leave your equipment in a parked car – and if you do have to, make sure that it's out of sight. Never leave a guitar on the back shelf, where it can be both clearly seen and exposed to direct sunlight. When you're driving, keep your guitar on the back seat, which doesn't get as cold (or as hot) as the boot/trunk.

Planes

If you're flying with your guitar or bass, it's best to carry it as hand luggage. If the airline won't allow this, try to check the guitar on as a fragile item.

10. AMPS AND EFFECTS

An electric guitar or bass only sounds its best when put through a decent amp, and for many players effects are also essential. This chapter tells you what you need to know about turning the sound of your instrument into the sound you want.

A major factor when buying an amp is what power rating to go for. Practice amps, suitable for playing at home, are as little as 10–20 watts, but you can get amps of several hundred watts.

RMS

There are various ways of measuring wattage (electrical power). For guitar amps the RMS system is normally used, so a '50-watt guitar amp' will have a power output of 50 watts RMS. (However, this may be much louder than a hi-fi amplifier of '50 watts', because hi-fi equipment is often measured with a different system, such as PMPO.) Don't confuse the power output with the power the amp uses. A 100 watt RMS bass amp, for example, may have a power consumption of 350 watts – but the power consumption tells you what it uses, not what it produces.

How much power?

Small practice amps are available from about £75/$100, and often have a headphone socket. If you play with a band you'll need more power, and that means spending more money. For a decent 50 watt amp, loud enough for most situations, expect to spend around £250/$350. Bassists need more power than guitarists because producing low-range pitches requires more energy. 100 watts should be enough to make your bass heard in a practice room.

PA systems

When you see a band play a large gig, the guitar and bass amps usually have a microphone in front of them. This is because the amplifiers themselves are amplified, and put through the overall speaker system that the singer goes through – the *PA system*. This is both to provide more volume and to allow the sound to be balanced. So you don't necessarily need an enormous amp to play an enormous gig.

Combos, heads and cabs

To amplify a guitar or bass you need two components: an electrical amplifier and one or more speakers. Any amp that has these two components together in one unit – as do most low-power and some high-power amps – is known as a *combo*. However, some powerful amps have a separate *head* (the amplifier) and *cabinet* (a box that just holds speakers). Some players use two or more cabinets, or *cabs*, with one head.

Quality

The power rating is one thing that affects the price of an amp, but the quality of the sound is also a major factor. A high-quality 50-watt amplifier can easily cost five times as much as a basic model of the same power. For the extra money you should get better speakers, electronics and build quality, and therefore a better sound.

Transistors and tubes

Most guitar amps use one of two systems to amplify sound: *transistors* (which are also used in hi-fi amps) or *tubes* (also known as *valves*). Tube amps are usually said to create a warmer and more lifelike sound, but they tend to be much more expensive than transistor (*solid state*) amps. There are also a growing number of *digital amplifiers* on the market, which emulate the sound of transistor and tube amps.

Character

A guitar amp does more than just amplify the sound of the instrument. It also gives your sound a certain character:

play the same guitar through two different amps and you get two different sounds. Of course, bass amps add colour to the sound too, but bass players generally go for a cleaner type of amplification than guitarists.

Speakers

Speakers (or *cones*) come in many sizes and qualities. Many guitar combos use a 12" speaker, but some smaller ones use a 10" or even an 8". Some combos are stereo, using two speakers to add space and width to the sound – this is especially noticeable when using stereo effects such as *stereo chorus*.

Bass combos

You'll find a 12" speaker in many bass combos, too, but bigger models often have a 15". Some have smaller speakers but more of them – after all, four 10" speakers move more air than two 12" speakers. Many bass combos have a *tweeter*, a small speaker to give extra definition to the high frequencies.

Cabinets

Cabinets come in a wide range of designs with many different arrangements of speakers. A popular type for guitarists is one with four 12" cones, whilst bass cabinets come with speakers as big as 18".

Channels

Many guitar players use some kind of distortion or over drive to give their sound some extra bite. Most guitar amps come with two or more *channels*: one for a clean sound, and the other(s) for a distorted sound. The clean channel is often called *rhythm*, because it's most commonly used for chord playing, whilst the distorted channels have names like *crunch*, *lead* or *drive*, and are often used for playing solo. Amps often come with pedals to allow you to change between channels whilst playing.

EQs

Most bass amps have no built-in effects, because bassists tend to want a clean sound. However, they often do come with extended tone controls – *equalizers* or *EQs* – which allow the accurate adjustment of different frequency bands.

Some also have a built-in *limiter* or *compressor*, which helps to limit the difference in volume between slapped, plucked and 'regular' notes.

EFFECTS

Distortion is one of the main effects used by guitarists. Another one is *reverb*, and most guitar amps have that built-in too. These effects and loads of others are available as single effect pedals, in multi-effect processors and in rack-mounted units.

Pedals

An effect pedal is a small box with a single pedal and a couple of controls, powered by a battery or an adapter. Prices range from about £35–175/$50–250, depending on the effect, the brand and the specifications. Some of the most popular types are described below.

Distortion

There's a wide range of distortion pedals available, which offer various different types and degrees of distortion. They often have names such as Metal, Smokin', Grunge or Rock. Fuzz boxes, crunchers, boosters and overdrives also create distortion, and most of them can also make your notes last however long you want. There are also special distortion pedals for creating and controlling feedback.

Chorus, reverb and delay

A *chorus* pedal gives you a full sound, as if each note were being simultaneously played on more than one instrument; this effect is used by both guitarists and bassists. *Reverb* is another very popular effect, making it sound like you're playing in a hall or church. *Delay* pedals create a kind of echo, but not the sort that occurs naturally. You can set the *delay time* (the echo length) and the pedal repeats whatever you play as many times as you like. With a short delay time the sound is a bit thicker, with a long delay time you can actually play over the top of what you just played.

Controls

Every effects pedal has a foot switch to turn it on or off plus a number of controls. If you have a delay pedal, for instance, you can use the controls to adjust the volume of the echo, how often you hear the echo, how long you hear it for, and the delay time – from thousandths of a second to a whole second or more.

Wah-wahs

There are also units where you don't only use the pedal to turn an effect on or off, but to actually control it. The most popular example is the *wah-wah* pedal, which creates a 'wah' sound when you press it down; the further you press it, the more intense the effect. *Volume pedals* look quite similar, and allow you to increase and decrease your overall volume.

Linking pedals

You can connect up a whole array of effect pedals one after the other, and there are special short leads available for going between them. However, a series of linked, separate devices is pretty unwieldy, so some players fix them all to a board. Ready-made *pedal boards* are even more elegant, and they usually come with a single power supply to save you having to use batteries or a separate adapter for each pedal.

Multi-effects

A multi-effect processor is a single unit that contains a number of effects, which can be mixed or used individually. Most have a number of pedals and a programming function, so you can spend ages designing the perfect sounds at home, and then turn them on with one touch on stage. Multi-effect processors often come with a built-in

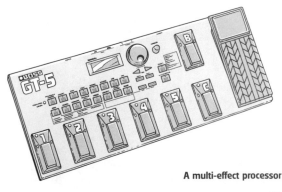

A multi-effect processor

tuner, a metronome and a headphone socket, so you can tune and practice in private. They start at around £100/$150, and go up in price offering better effects, more effects, less hiss and more functions. Some even include a large pedal for wah-wah and volume control.

Rack units

Effects and multi-effects are also sold in rack-mountable units, which are usually quite expensive. Most are 19" wide (to fit in the standard studio rack) and their height is given in numbers of rack units.

11. BACK IN TIME

The solid-body guitar and the bass guitar have only been around since the 1950s, but in half a century have established themselves as among the most important instruments for loads of musical styles. This chapter gives an outline of their history.

Stringed instruments have been around for millennia – and the guitar has ancestors dating back to the ancient Greek lyre played in myth by Orpheus. The electric guitar's more recent parentage lies with the acoustic guitar, which itself evolved from many instruments, including the medieval lute, the Moorish guitar and the Arabic *oud*.

The lute

The lute was the most popular stringed instrument in Renaissance Europe and acoustic guitar makers are still called *luthiers*. However, the first instruments that resembled today's guitar emerged in the sixteenth century; they generally had five single or double strings.

The classical guitar

Some time between 1850 and 1860 the Spaniard Antonio de Torres Jurado built an instrument close to today's classical guitar in terms of shape, sound and construction. Gut was used for classical guitar strings until around 1950, when it was replaced by nylon.

The steel-string guitar

Around the same time that Torres was working on his instruments in Europe, American guitar maker George

Friedrich Martin was creating the forerunners of the modern steel-string acoustic guitar. He designed the larger sound-box and *X-bracing* (a method of constructing guitar tops).

Blues and jazz

Blues music developed at the end of the nineteenth century in the US, and the earliest singers of the style would often accompany themselves on guitars. Blues is one of the fore-runners of jazz, and most jazz bands, including the early ones, depended on drums, trumpets and saxophones as well as guitars. And since those instruments are pretty loud, guitars had to be made louder too.

Archtops

The early jazz guitarists opted for the American-designed archtop guitar, with a hollow body, an arched top with *f*-shaped soundholes, and steel strings – all of which helped to produce greater volume. And it was the archtop that was first fitted with pickups, some time in the 1930s. Many jazz guitarists today still use similar models to the ones from that period.

Solid-bodies

Around twenty years later, Leo Fender designed the first solid-body electric guitar to be mass-produced. It was originally called the Fender Broadcaster but was soon re-named the Telecaster. This model is still being built, and many brands have made instruments based on its design.

The Strat and Les Paul

The next major development was the Fender Stratocaster – the 'Strat' – which arrived in 1954, and the Gibson Les Paul, a solid-body designed by the jazz guitarist Les Paul. These guitars are not only still being produced, but are perhaps the two most popular models in the world, and have inspired endless other instruments.

Bass guitars

After Leo Fender produced his first solid-body guitars, he realized he could build bass guitars the same way. And just like his first guitars, his original bass design – the Fender Precision – remains one of the most popular models available today.

Advantages

Fender's electric bass had numerous advantages over its predecessor, the double bass. It was much more portable, it allowed players to produce more volume, and, because it had frets, it was much easier to learn to play in tune. Also, because it was so like the guitar, it made it easy for guitarists to double as bass players.

Since then

Many of the most popular guitars and basses used today are based on the classic instruments from the 1950s, but lots of new inventions and thousands of new models have been designed since then. Active electronics and pickups with less hum, for example, and new materials for necks and bodies, like plastics and graphite. Better frets have also been developed, as have strings that sound clearer and last longer. And, of course, countless new body shapes have been designed – although guitars with 'special' bodies, such as the Gibson Explorer and the Gibson Flying V have actually been around since the 1950s. Lots of variations on the standard instruments have also evolved, such as those with extra necks, no head or more strings. For more details about these, go on to the next chapter.

A Gibson Flying V from 1958

12. THE GUITAR FAMILY

The electric guitar and bass are related to all other in-struments that use strings to make their sound, such as the harp and violin. This chapter only deals with close relatives – the guitar family – from the classical guitar to the violin bass and the midi-guitar.

There are thousands of ways to build a guitar or bass, and there's often quite a lot of confusion about what each type is called. The following pages should clarify things a little. First, we'll divide the guitar family into two main groups and five subgroups.

Acoustic guitars:
- The **classical guitar** has a relatively small resonance chamber and uses nylon strings. It's mostly used for classical guitar music and is also called the *Spanish guitar* or *nylon-string guitar*.
- The **steel-string guitar** has steel strings and a larger soundbox than the classical guitar. It's mainly used for strumming chords, and is also known as the *folk guitar* or *western guitar*.
- The **electro-acoustic guitar** is an acoustic guitar with a built-in pickup.

Electric guitars:
- The **solid-body** has a solid body instead of a soundbox.
- A **hollow-body** is an electric guitar with a soundbox. Depending on the size of the soundbox, various other names are used such as full-body, jazz guitar, slimline, thinline, semi-acoustic or semi-solid.

Steel-string guitars

Unlike classical guitars, which all have roughly the same dimensions, steel-string guitars come in numerous shapes and sizes. The two best-known large body-shapes are the *Dreadnought*, named after an old battleship, and the *Jumbo*.

Flattops

The vast majority of steel-string guitars have a flat top, and those that do are referred to as *flattops*. Classical guitars always have flat tops, but the term flattop isn't applied to them.

Find out more

If you want to know more about acoustic guitars, read *The Rough Guide to Acoustic Guitar*.

SOLID-BODY VARIATIONS

There's an incredibly wide variety of solid-body guitars and basses available, including some with weird body shapes, unusual artwork, extra strings and even extra necks.

The Ibanez IC 350

Double-necks

There are various types of guitars with two necks. Most have one six-string and one twelve-string neck, although some have one guitar neck and one bass neck. There are even instruments with more than two necks – guitars with five have been built.

More strings

Electric twelve-string guitars are less common than acoustic ones, but they're by no means rare. There are also *ten-string guitars*, on which the four top strings are doubled

A Gibson with one six-string neck and one twelve-string neck

to provide a richer sound. Another variation – one that became increasingly popular in the 1990s – is the *seven-string guitar*, which usually has an additional low A- or B-string. There are both electric and acoustic seven-strings available.

Multi-string basses

Twelve-string electric basses have two guitar strings next to each bass string, so each note sounds like it's being played simultaneously on a guitar and a bass. Five- and six-string basses are much more common. Usually, those with five strings have either a low B or a high C in addition to the normal four, and those with six strings have both. Occasionally, you may come across a seven- or even eight-string bass.

The Hamer Chapparal, a twelve-string bass guitar

Woodless and headless

In the early Eighties, Ned Steinberger developed a bass guitar that had the machine heads at the tail, making the headstock redundant. This design paved the way for many headless instruments, both basses and guitars. Also, Steinberger substituted wood for a reinforced glass and carbon-fibre resin.

The Steinberger headless bass

Unusual bodies

There are endless ways to shape the body of an electric guitar or bass. Three striking designs are shown below: the Höfner Violin Bass (with a hollow, violin-shaped body), the Washburn EC36 (with 36 frets and a handle built into the body), and the aggressive-looking Jackson Professional Warrior.

The Höfner Violin Bass

The Washburn EC36

The Jackson Professional Warrior

MIDI

Instruments with MIDI (which stands for Musical Instrument Digital Interface) can be hooked up to each other and to computers. With a MIDI guitar you can operate a drum machine, for example, or play with a saxophone sound from a keyboard. The Roland G-707 was one of the first MIDI guitars.

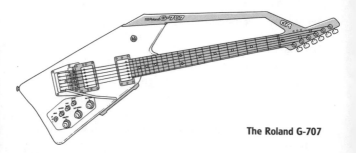

The Roland G-707

Built-in amps

Some manufacturers produced guitars with amplifiers and speakers built into the body. The idea never really caught on, but you do see these instruments around occasionally.

ELECTRO-ACOUSTICS

Most electro-acoustic guitars and basses are essentially regular steel-string acoustics with a built-in pickup. They use a so-called *piezo* or *piezo-electric pickup*, which is usually located in the bridge, under the saddle.

Controls

Volume and tone controls are usually found on an electro-acoustic guitar's shoulder (or *upper bout*). The control

An electro-acoustic Dreadnought with a cutaway

panel often includes various other features, including a battery-check LED, for the battery that powers the built-in pre-amp.

A control panel on an electro-acoustic guitar

Nylon strings

Unlike the magnetic pickups on electric guitars, piezo pickups work with nylon strings, too, and there are quite a lot of nylon-string electro-acoustic guitars around. They often have smaller and thinner bodies than their fully acoustic counterparts, and many have cutaways.

Semi-solids

Some nylon-string electro-acoustics have a shallow body and one or more hidden resonance chambers. This type – which you can also get with steel strings – is said to play and sound like an acoustic guitar, but have all the advantages of an electric guitar. They're usually referred to as *semi-solids* (although semi-acoustic and other names are also used) and are manufactured by brands such as Godin.

The Godin Acousticaster

AND MORE

There are, of course, many other instruments that belong to the electric guitar and bass family. The slide guitar, for example, which is rested flat on a table or your lap and played with a slide. The Chapman Stick is another relative, which has been around since the mid-1970s. It has ten or twelve strings that the player taps with both hands – similar to the tapping technique used by some guitarists and bassists.

13. HOW THEY'RE MADE

If you want to know more about guitars and basses, it's good to have an idea of how they're made. Here's a brief introduction to guitar and bass construction.

The body of a solid-body instrument often looks as though it's made from a single piece of wood – but that's hardly ever the case. Many are built from two or more pieces, some from layers of wood (laminated bodies), and others from synthetic materials, which are becoming ever more popular.

Book-matched bodies

Many instruments have *book-matched bodies*, which are made by sawing a single piece of wood into two pieces and opening it up like a book. The two halves – which are the mirror image of each other – are then glued together. As well as looking good, book-matched bodies are highly resistant to warping.

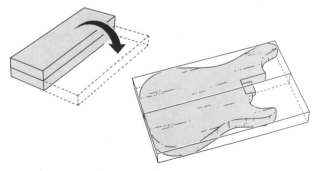

Making a book-matched solid-body

Woodwork and finish

Once the wooden sections are glued together, the desired shape can be cut out. The corners are then rounded off and holes are drilled for the electronics and hardware. When the body is the right shape it's stained or painted as necessary and then given many layers of varnish or lacquer. Some guitars are finished with wax.

The neck and fretboard

Like the body, the neck is often made from more than one piece of wood, and on most guitars and basses the fretboard is a separate piece. The neck is glued or screwed (or both) to the body, except with through-neck instruments, for which two wing-shaped pieces are attached to an extended neck.

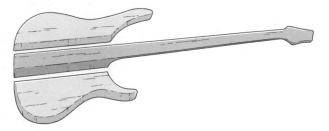

Making a through-neck instrument

Hardware

Once the woodwork is finished the pickups, wires, switches, machine heads, bridge, nut and other hardware are mounted. And, last of all, the strings are fitted.

Hollow-bodies

A decent hollow-body is more expensive than a solid-body of the same quality, largely because building a soundbox is a more complicated and time-consuming process than making a solid body. The sides (or *ribs*) of the soundbox are soaked in water, bent using heat, and then clamped in a mould. Where they meet the top on the inside, *linings* are used to strengthen the join.

14. THE BRANDS

There are thousands of guitar companies and individual makers – just a list of their names would fill a book of this size. This chapter introduces some of the most important brands and gives an idea of their price ranges.

There are more guitar brands than there are factories, since many factories (especially those in Taiwan and Korea) produce parts and complete instruments for various different brands. In fact, if you order a substantial number of instruments, getting your own brand on the market can take as little as a few weeks.

 The American company Fender was the first manufacturer to build solid-body guitars and basses. Today, Fender guitars are manufactured in a number of different countries, including China, Korea, Japan and Mexico, often under the Squier name. The most expensive Fenders, though, are still built in the US.

 Gibson guitars were founded in America in 1902. Thirty years after that, the factory built its first semi-acoustic guitar, the Electric Spanish Guitar. Gibson's first solid-body was the Les Paul, which was first made in 1952 and is still in production today. Gibson guitars are found in the high price ranges, but the company's sub-brand Epiphone produces less expensive instruments.

Ibanez Founded in Japan, Ibanez produce guitars in pretty much every price range. Unlike Fender and Gibson, the company doesn't use a different brand name for its cheaper guitars. Ibanez instruments are especially popular with rock guitarists.

WASHBURN Washburn is an American company that makes guitars and a wide range of other string instruments. **PEAVEY** Peavey, also from the US, manufacture amps and cabinets as well **YAMAHA** as guitars and basses. Yamaha, a huge Japanese corporation, produces a wide variety of guitars and other musical instruments as well as motorcycles, hi-fi equipment, boats and more.

OTHER BRANDS

Many of the inexpensive brands – such as Aria, Cort, Encore, Hohner, Samick, Tokai and Vantage – produce instruments in Asian countries. Some of these companies also offer more expensive guitars or make the cheaper 'import' ranges for big-name brands.

High-budget

There are just as many companies that only make high-budget guitars and basses. These manufacturers tend to produce instruments with distinctive designs, which are crafted by hand to a greater extent and feature more expensive components and wood types. Some examples are Blade, Patrick Eggle, Hamer, Jackson, Godin, Gretsch, Music Man, Rickenbacker and Paul Reed Smith. Some of these brands also produce basses, whilst other manufacturers – such as Alembic, Bogart, G&L, Spector, Status, Tobias and Warwick – specialize in basses.

Custom

Besides all of these, there are a great deal of custom guitar builders – usually one-man companies that produce only a few guitars or basses per year. Every piece is hand-made exactly to the customer's wishes. Not surprisingly, though, these instruments don't come cheap.

Accessories

There are also companies that don't make guitars at all, but concentrate on pickups, machine heads and other components. Some of the best-known pickup makers include Joe Barden, Bartolini, EMG, Evans, Seymour Duncan and DiMarzio. Major producers of machine heads include Gotoh, Grover, Kluson, Schaller and Sperzel. Their products tend to be found only on expensive instruments, or those that have been customized.

GLOSSARY AND INDEX

This glossary briefly explains all the terms you'll find in this book, and other jargon you may come across as a player. The numbers refer to the page(s) that contain more information on each subject.

10:1, 12:1, 14:1 *(35)* Turning a 10:1 machine head ten times makes the string post rotate once. A 14:1 machine requires fourteen turns for one rotation, allowing for more accurate tuning.

Acoustic *(88)* An acoustic guitar or bass has a hollow body (also called a 'sound-box' or 'resonance chamber') and can be played without amplification.

Action *(26, 69–72)* The distance between the strings and the fretboard; also referred to as 'string height'.

Active *(33)* Active guitars and basses use active electronics with a built-in pre-amplifier that boosts the signal before sending it to the main amp. Most gui-

tars and basses have a non-active, or 'passive', system.

Adjustments See: *Set up.*

Archtop *(9, 86)* Any guitar with an arched top. The term is most commonly used to describe hollow-body guitars, but is also used for solid-bodies with arched tops.

Binding *(10)* A decorative and protective strip that runs around the edge of an instrument's body. Some guitars and basses also have binding on the neck and headstock.

Boiling *(73–74)* A trick for cleaning bass strings.

Book-matched *(95)* A book-matched body consists

of two symmetrical halves cut from a single piece of wood. Hollow-body tops are also usually book-matched.

Booster *(82)* A guitar effect.

Box Another name for a hollow-body's soundbox.

Bridge *(7, 32, 49, 70)* The metal component on the body with the saddles on it. On most solid-bodies the strings are also attached to the bridge.

Bridge pickup *(52)* The pickup closest to the bridge; also called 'lead pickup'.

Bridge saddles See: *Saddles.*

Camber See: *Radius.*

Capo *(67)* A clamp that can be attached to a guitar's neck at any fret, raising the overall pitch of the instrument in semitones/ half-steps.

Chorus *(81)* A guitar effect.

Classical guitar *(85, 88)* An acoustic guitar with nylon strings; also called 'Spanish guitar'.

Coils *(52–53, 57, 75)* Magnets with thin copper wire wound around them. Each pickup uses either one or two coils. See also: *Single-coil pickup* and *Humbucker.*

Coil-tap *(54)* With a coil-tap, you can make a humbucker act like a single-coil pickup.

Combo *(80, 81)* An amplifier and speaker in a single casing; also called *speaker-amp.*

Compound radius *(26)* See: *Radius.*

Cord See: *Leads.*

Cordless system *(51)* A system that beams the signal from a guitar to an amp instead of using a lead.

Cruncher *(82)* A guitar effect.

Cutaway *(5)* A section cut out from the lower shoulder to allow easier access to the high frets. On many instruments the upper shoulder is also cut away.

Delay *(82)* A guitar effect.

Distortion *(81)* A guitar effect.

Double-coil pickup *(52–53, 55, 57, 75)* A pickup with two coils, such as a humbucker. See also: *Humbucker.*

Double-neck *(89)* A guitar or bass with two necks.

Dreadnought *(89, 92)* See: *Steel-string guitar.*

D-tuner *(68)* A device that allows you to detune the low E-string down to D at the touch of a button.

Effect pedal *(77, 82–83)* A small, foot-operated device used to change the sound of your instrument. See also: *Multi-effect processor.*

Electro-acoustic guitar *(88, 92–93)* Usually a steel-string acoustic guitar with a piezo pickup built into the bridge. You can also get nylon-string and bass electro-acoustics.

Equalizers *(81)* An extensive set of tone controls, often found on bass amps; also called 'EQs' and 'graphic equalizers'.

Face See: *Top.*

Feedback *(10)* A pickup sends the sound of a guitar to an amplifier, which then sends it to a speaker. Sometimes, the pickup 'picks up' its own sound from the speaker, and so sends the same sound back to the amplifier, which then sends it back to the speaker again.

This goes round and round causing a loud piercing screech known as feedback. Hollow-body guitars create worse feedback than solid-bodies.

ƒ-hole *(9, 86)* A soundhole in the shape of an 'ƒ', found on most hollow-body guitars as well as on violins, cellos, etc.

Fine-tuners, fine-machine heads *(36)* Devices on the bridge used for tuning. Found on guitars with locking nuts.

Fingerboard See: *Fretboard.*

Five-string bass *(90)* The extra string is usually a low B, but sometimes a high C or another pitch.

Flattop *(89)* A steel-string guitar with a flat top and a hollow body. See also: *Archtop.*

Flat-wound *(41–42)* A string wound with flat wire.

Fretboard *(5, 6, 25–26, 30–31, 37, 69, 74)* The part of the neck with the frets on it; also called *fingerboard.*

Fretless bass *(32)* A bass guitar without frets.

Frets *(5, 27–28, 32, 38, 43, 71, 74, 87)* The metal strips on the fretboard.

Full-body *(88)* A hollow-body guitar with a large soundbox; full-bodies are also called jazz guitars.

Fuzz box *(82)* A guitar effect pedal.

Gig bag *(76)* A padded bag for carrying a guitar or bass.

Ground-wound *(41)* See: *Round-wound.*

Half-round *(41)* See: *Round-wound.*

Hardware *(19)* The metal components of a guitar, including the bridge and machine heads.

Harmonics *(63–65, 66, 72)* Notes produced when striking a string that's lightly touched above certain frets, including the twelfth (the middle of the string), the seventh (a third of the string), the fifth (a quarter of the string). Harmonics are sometimes called 'overtones' or 'flageolets', and are useful for tuning.

Head, headstock *(6–7, 24, 31, 90)* The section at the top of the neck which holds the machine heads.

Headless instruments *(90–91)* Guitars and basses without a head.

Hollow-body *(8–9, 21, 22, 25, 29, 48, 70, 88, 96)* An electric guitar with a hollow body. See also: *Solid-body* and *Archtop.*

Horn *(4)* The pointed section of a body that's left by cutting out a cutaway.

Hum See: *Interference.*

Humbucker *(52–54, 57, 75)* A kind of double-coil pickup designed to reduce unwanted humming (to 'buck the hum'). However, the term is often used to describe any double-coil pickups. Humbuckers sound thicker and warmer than single-coil pickups.

Insurance *(77)* You can extend your home insurance to cover your guitar or bass equipment, or take out a separate policy.

Interference *(38, 51, 56, 75)* Electrical effect that causes humming, squeaking, crackling and other unwanted noises.

Intonation *(49, 72)* If the intonation of a guitar or bass is correct, a string played at the twelfth fret is exactly one octave higher than when it's played open. Intonation can be adjusted by moving the saddles.

Jack, jack plug, jack lead *(9)* The jack is the type of plug used on guitar leads, and the leads themselves are often referred to as 'jack leads'.

Jazz guitar *(9, 88)* Usually a hollow-body electric guitar with a relatively deep soundbox.

Jumbo See: *Steel-string guitar.*

Leads *(51, 75)* The wires used for connecting a guitar or bass to an amplifier; also called 'cords', 'cables' and 'jack leads'.

Left-handed *(10)* Left-handed instruments are quite common, but not all left-handed players use them.

Locking machine heads *(34, 48)* Machine heads which 'lock' the strings in place.

Locking nut, lock-nut *(36, 37)* A clamp that fixes the strings at the nut to prevent them detuning from the use of a tremolo; also called 'top-lock'.

Long scale See: *Scale.*

Machine heads *(7, 34–35, 37, 47–48, 64, 90)* The devices on the headstock that the strings are attached to, and which are used to tighten and loosen the strings; also called 'tuners', 'tuning heads', 'tuning machines', 'tuning keys' and 'tuning gears'.

Markers See: *Position markers.*

Medium scale See: *Scale.*

Metronome *(17)* A small device that ticks or bleeps out a steady, adjustable pulse, helping you to work on tempo, timing and rhythm.

MIDI *(92)* Musical Instrument Digital Interface. MIDI instruments can be connected to each other and to computers.

Multi-effect processor *(82–83)* A device (usually programmable) that offers two or more effects.

Neck *(5, 25, 30, 31, 43, 67, 71, 96)* The section of a guitar that runs between the body and the head.

Neck pickup *(52)* The pickup closest to the neck; also called 'rhythm pickup'.

Nut *(7, 32, 43, 65, 70)* A small strip, usually made out of plastic, which the strings run over at the end of the fretboard. It keeps the strings at the correct distance from each other and the right height above the fretboard.

Open tuning *(67)* A way of tuning a guitar.

Overdrive *(81, 82)* A guitar effect.

PA system *(80)* The main amp and speaker system used at a gig (from the term public address). The guitar and bass amps are often re-amplified through the PA.

Passive See: *Active.*

Pedal board *(83)* A box or board used to arrange, store and power any number of effects pedals.

Pick *(5, 49–51)* Usually a triangular piece of plastic used to strum the strings. Playing with a pick produces a sharper sound than playing with fingertips. Picks are also called 'plectrums'.

Pickguard *(5)* A plastic panel that protects a section of the body from being scratched by picks. On solid-body instruments, removing the pickguard often gives access to the electronics inside. Pickguards are also called 'scratch plates'.

Pickup *(3, 7, 29, 33, 38, 52–57)* A special type of magnet which picks up the vibrations of the strings and converts them into electrical signals.

Pickup selector, pickup switch *(7, 38, 55–56)* Switch for choosing between the pickups on an instrument; also called 'toggle switch'.

Piezo pickup *(92–93)* Type of pickup used on electro-acoustic guitars and basses.

Plain strings *(39, 42, 47)* The two or three plain wire (not wound) strings on a guitar. See also: *Wound strings.*

Plectrum See: *Pick.*

Plug See: *Jack.*

Position *(6, 11–12, 69)* The section between two frets. 'Playing in the third position' means playing at the third fret.

Position markers *(6)* Dots or patterns on the front and side of the fretboard to help the player quickly find the right fret. The twelfth fret (the octave) often has a double dot or extra-large marker.

Post See: *String post.*

Pot, potentiometer 'Technicians' jargon for the kind of electrical controls found under the volume and tone knobs of a guitar or bass.

Prices *(21–22)*

Radius *(25–26)* The fretboard's curvature; also called *camber.* Most fretboards are higher in the middle (under the middle strings) that at the edges (under the outer strings). The bigger the curve, the smaller the radius number. A fretboard with a *compound radius* is more curved at the nut than at the last fret.

Resonance chamber See: *Soundbox.*

Reverb *(82)* A guitar effect.

Round-wound *(41–42)* A string wound with a thin, round wire. 'Groundwounds' and 'half-rounds' are round-wounds that have been filed a little flatter – but they're not as flat as flat-wounds.

Saddles *(7, 35, 43, 70–72)* The small devices that the strings run over at the bridge. The saddles determine the length, height and (sometimes) spacing of the strings. They're sometimes called 'bridge saddles'.

Scale *(27)* The distance between the saddles and the nut; also referred to as 'speaking length' because this is the section of the string that vibrates to create a note.

Scratch plate See: *Pickguard.*

Secondhand buying tips *(22–23, 37–38)*

Semi-acoustic *(9, 88)* A guitar with one or more pickups and a soundbox. The term is usually applied to hollow-bodies (especially those with a shallow soundbox) but is also used to refer to electro-acoustics.

Semi-solid *(88, 93)* A guitar that looks like a solid-body, but has one or more small resonance chambers inside the body.

Set up *(20, 69–70, 72)* Setting up a guitar involves carefully adjusting the action, intonation and pickups, to make an instrument play and sound better.

Short scale See: *Scale.*

Single-coil pickup *(52–55, 73, 75)* A pickup with one coil. Single-coils have a brighter sound than double-coils. See also: *Double-coil pickup* and *Humbucker.*

Six-string bass *(89)* The two extra strings are usually a low B and a high C.

Slanted body A type of body with an asymmetrical lower half; also referred to as *asymmetrical body* or *offset waist.*

Slimline See: *Thinline.*

Solid-body An electric guitar or bass with a solid body.

Solo pickup See: *Bridge pickup.*

Soundbox *(3, 9, 21, 29, 86, 88, 96)* A hollow body that acoustically amplifies the sound of a guitar or bass. Also referred to as 'resonance chamber' or 'sound chamber'.

Soundhole *(9, 86)* A hole in the top of a soundbox. Archtops often have *f*-shaped soundholes, whilst most flattops and classical guitars have round ones.

Speaker-amp See: *Combo.*

Speaking length See: *Scale.*

Split pickup *(55)* A single-coil pickup in two parts, most commonly used on bass guitars.

Steel-string guitar *(85–86, 88, 89, 92)* An acoustic guitar with steel strings; also called 'folk guitar' and 'western guitar'. Popular models include the Jumbo and the Dreadnought.

A steel-string guitar with a built-in pickup

Stratitis, string-pull *(73)* Guitar 'disease' caused

mainly by single-coil pick-ups.

String post *(7, 47)* The section of a machine head that a string actually winds around.

String tree *(8, 48, 49)* A device on the headstock that holds down the thinner strings so that they don't pop out of the nut.

String winder *(44–45)* A plastic device that speeds up the process of winding and unwinding strings.

Strings *(39–49, 71–72)*. See pages 43–49 for changing strings.

Sunburst A finish that is brighter in the middle of the body than at the edges.

Sunburst finish

Sustain *(28)* How long a sound lasts for. The longer it lasts, the longer the sustain.

Tailpiece *(7, 49)* On most hollow-bodies and some

solid-bodies the strings are attached to a tailpiece instead of at the bridge.

Thinline *(9, 88)* A hollow-body guitar with a shallow soundbox; also called 'slim-line'.

Through-neck *(30, 96)* A neck that extends through the body to the tail.

Toggle switch See: *Pickup selector.*

Tone controls *(7, 81, 92)* Knobs for altering the tone of a guitar or bass.

Top *(9, 29–30, 89)* The top of a guitar's body; also called the 'face'.

Top-lock *(36)* See: *Locking nut.*

Transducer See: *Pickup.*

Tremolo system *(9–10, 35–37, 41, 48, 64, 71)* A kind of bridge with a small 'arm' that allows you to alter the tension of a guitar's strings, bending the pitch up or down. Also called *whammy bar* and *vibrato* (which is one of the effects you actually produce with a tremolo arm).

Truss rod *(5, 26, 71)* A metal rod running through

the neck, preventing it from warping under the tension of the strings. Electric guitars and basses usually have an adjustable truss rod.

Tuner *(44, 65–66)* An electronic device to make tuning easier and more accurate; also called 'electronic tuner'. However, tuner is also another name for a machine head. See also: *Machine heads.*

Tuning fork *(59–66)* A two-pronged metal fork, which creates a note to tune to. Usually available for the notes A, E and C.

Tuning machines See: *Machine heads.*

Vibrato See: *Tremolo system.*

Volume control *(7, 35, 56)* Knob for altering the volume on a guitar or bass.

Wah-wah *(83, 84)* A guitar effect.

Western guitar Another name for a steel-string guitar. See: *Steel-string guitar.*

Whammy, whammy bar See: *Tremolo system.*

Wound strings *(39, 42, 43, 47, 73)* Strings wound with thin metal wire so they can produce better low notes. The thickest three or four guitar strings and all bass strings are wound.

Zero fret *(32)* An extra fret right next to the nut, designed to make open strings sound more similar to fretted strings.

WANT TO KNOW MORE?

This book gives you all the basics you need for buying, maintaining and using an electric guitar or bass. If you want to know more, try the magazines, books, Web sites and newsgroups listed below.

MAGAZINES

Some of these magazines specifically deal with electric guitars (or basses) while others cover acoustics too. Some deal with a certain style of guitar music.

UK

- *Guitarist* www.guitarist.co.uk
- *Guitar Techniques* www.guitartechniques.co.uk
- *The Guitar Magazine* www.linkhouse.co.uk/guitar.html
- *Total Guitar* www.totalguitar.co.uk

US

- *Bass Frontiers* www.bassfrontiers.com
- *Bass Player* www.bassplayer.com
- *Bassics* www.bassics.com
- *Guitar* www.guitarmag.com
- *Guitar Player* www.guitarplayer.com
- *Guitar Review* www.guitarreview.com
- *Guitar World* www.guitarworld.com

BOOKS

Countless books have been written about guitars. The three below are good supplements to this guide:

- *The Complete Guitarist*, Richard Chapman (Dorling Kindersley, UK/US). Beautiful photographs, historical overview, playing tips, tuning tips, practicing, amplification and background information. Not for bassists.

- *The Ultimate Guitar Book,* Tony Bacon (Dorling Kindersley, UK/US). Focuses on the instrument and not on playing it. Includes many full-colour photos and information about basses, acoustics and semi-acoustics.
- *The New Guitar Handbook,* Ralph Denyer (Pan, UK); *The Guitar Handbook,* Ralph Denyer (Knopf, US). Historical and up-to-date information about electric and acoustic guitars, basses, amps and effects. Includes a basic playing course and profiles of influential guitarists.

THE INTERNET

The Internet offers a huge amount of information about guitars and basses. One of the easiest ways to discover what's there is to go to a site that offers lots of links to other sites, such as www.guitarsite.com and www.guitarist.com. Lots of brands have their own Web site, which you can often find by putting the brand's name between 'www.' and '.com' (for example, www.gibson.com or www.fender.com). You'll find lots of other sites by doing a Web-search for electric+guitar or bass+ guitar.

Newsgroups

You can pick up a lot of information in the various guitar newsgroups. Try rec.music.makers.guitar for a whole host of questions, answers, tips and articles written for and by guitarists and bassists. Others newsgroups focus on a particular style of playing (such as rec.music.makers.guitar jazz).

ESSENTIAL DATA

In the event of your equipment being stolen or lost, both the police and your insurance company will need certain information. Even if you just want to sell any of your gear, it's useful to have a note of the original price and specifications. You can use these pages to keep a record of all the relevant data.

INSURANCE

Insurance company:

Phone: Fax:

Contact person:

Phone: Fax:

Policy number:

Premium:

INSTRUMENTS AND ACCESSORIES

Make and model:

Serial number:

Specifications:

Purchase date:

Place of purchase:

Phone: Fax:

Make and model:

Serial number:

Specifications:

Purchase date:

Place of purchase:

Phone: Fax:

Make and model:

Serial number:

Specifications:

Purchase date:

Place of purchase:

Phone: Fax:

Make and model:

Serial number:

Specifications:

Purchase date:

Place of purchase:

Phone: Fax:

ADDITIONAL NOTES

....

....

....

....

....

....

....

....

....

....

....

....

....

....

....

....

....

ADDITIONAL NOTES